CHRISTMAS IS COMING! 1987

**Compiled and Edited
by Linda Martin Stewart**

Oxmoor
House®

Library of Congress Catalog Card Number:
84-63030

ISBN: 0-8487-0710-9
ISSN: 0883-9077

Manufactured in the United States of America
First Printing

Executive Editor: Candace N. Conard
Production Manager: Jerry Higdon
Associate Production Manager: Rick Litton
Art Director: Bob Nance

Christmas Is Coming! 1987

Editor: Linda Martin Stewart
Illustrator and Designer: Caroline Wellesley
Editorial Assistant: Lenda Wyatt
Copy Chief: Mary Jean Haddin
Photographers: Jim Bathie, Colleen Duffley

Contents

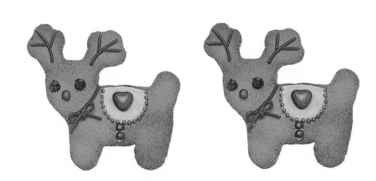

A Word to Parents

Here comes Christmas 1987, and amazingly enough, one box of last year's trimmings still sits in the corner of my bedroom, awaiting its return to the attic. Why I never made it up the pull-down stairs with this last box, I've forgotten. But since both it and the holidays are close at hand, I choose to think at this point, not that I'm a bit behind, but rather a step ahead!

Boasting extra pages and a brand new chapter, this year's edition of *Christmas Is Coming!* is bigger and better than ever. Go ahead—have a look inside. Choose a project, begin it—and you can claim a head start, too!

Making its debut in *Christmas Is Coming! 1987*, Kids in the Kitchen adds a dash of family fun. A mini-cookbook, this chapter is filled with recipes chosen especially with children and Christmas in mind.

You'll need an extra cookie jar once your kids get a taste of "Cookie Fun." Chock-full of recipes for cookies of all flavors, this section will be a winner with youngsters and grown-ups alike. And not to be outdone by "Cookie Fun," "Goodies and Gifts" offers both an assortment of tasty foods and an assortment of snappy ways to wrap them for presents.

Before donning their aprons and heading for the kitchen, kids will want to turn to Children's Workshop and take a peek at the rest of the fun that *Christmas Is Coming! 1987* has in store. An imaginative collection of Christmas crafts, Children's Workshop includes page after colorful page of trimmings to fix—ornaments, decorations, cards, and wraps—and presents to make.

As in the past, step-by-step illustrations, full-size patterns, and numbered instructions are included with each of the projects in Children's Workshop. As you look over these projects, notice that suggestions (Before You Start) or words of caution (For Safety's Sake) occasionally precede the instructions. Also note that at the bottom of the first page of each project, there is a level rating of 1, 2, or 3, with Level 1 indicating the quickest, easiest projects, and Level 3 the most difficult ones or those calling for adult supervision. The projects within Level 2 are easy, but call for minimal help from a grown-up, a certain skill, or extra time and patience. Please understand that these ratings are intended only as a guide. Because parents know their children's abilities best, I highly recommend that you look through these projects with your children and decide together which ones are suitable for them to make.

For the kids you love, only the best will do, and Parents' Workshop is packed with plenty of just that: the best in gift ideas for children. Appearing for the first time, "Hold It" features a satchel set, dinosaur peg rack, kitty-cat bookrack, and other handy gifts. Delightfully different ways to dress up kids' clothes abound in "Grin and Wear It," and in "Just for Fun," you'll find a range of cute and colorful gifts—from a jack-in-the-box lamp to a bowling pin set. And to keep the spirits of Santa's helpers merry, the projects in Parents' Workshop are presented similarly to those in Children's Workshop— with color photographs, full-size patterns, and step-by-step instructions.

Like a big Christmas stocking, *Christmas Is Coming! 1987* holds one nice surprise after another. May you and your children enjoy the contents.

Happy holidays!

Linda Martin Stewart

KIDS IN THE KITCHEN
A Christmas Cookbook

COOKIE FUN

Cookies, cookies, cookies! Bake a batch of each of these. See which ones you like the best!

Merry Christmas Cookies

¾ cup butter or margarine, softened
1 cup firmly packed brown sugar
1 egg yolk
2 cups all-purpose flour
1½ teaspoons ground cinnamon
½ teaspoon baking powder
¼ teaspoon salt
frosting (your favorite)
candies, raisins, and other decorations

1. Trace and cut out the patterns on the following page. Draw around the patterns on a piece of stiff paper. Cut out the patterns and set them aside.

2. In a large bowl, cream the butter. Add the sugar, a little at a time, and beat until light and fluffy. Add the egg yolk and beat well.

3. Mix the flour, cinnamon, baking powder, and salt. Add this mixture to the butter mixture and mix well.

4. Divide the dough in half and wrap each half in a piece of waxed paper. Chill the wrapped dough in the freezer for about thirty minutes.

5. Preheat the oven to 375°. Sprinkle your work surface lightly with flour. Roll half of the dough ⅛″ thick. Place the cookie patterns on the dough and cut around them with a knife.

6. Using a spatula, place the cookies 1″ apart on ungreased cookie sheets. Bake for 8 to 10 minutes or until light brown.

7. Let the cookies cool a few minutes. Move the cookies to a wire rack and let cool completely. Frost and decorate the cookies. Makes about 14 cookies.

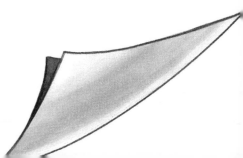

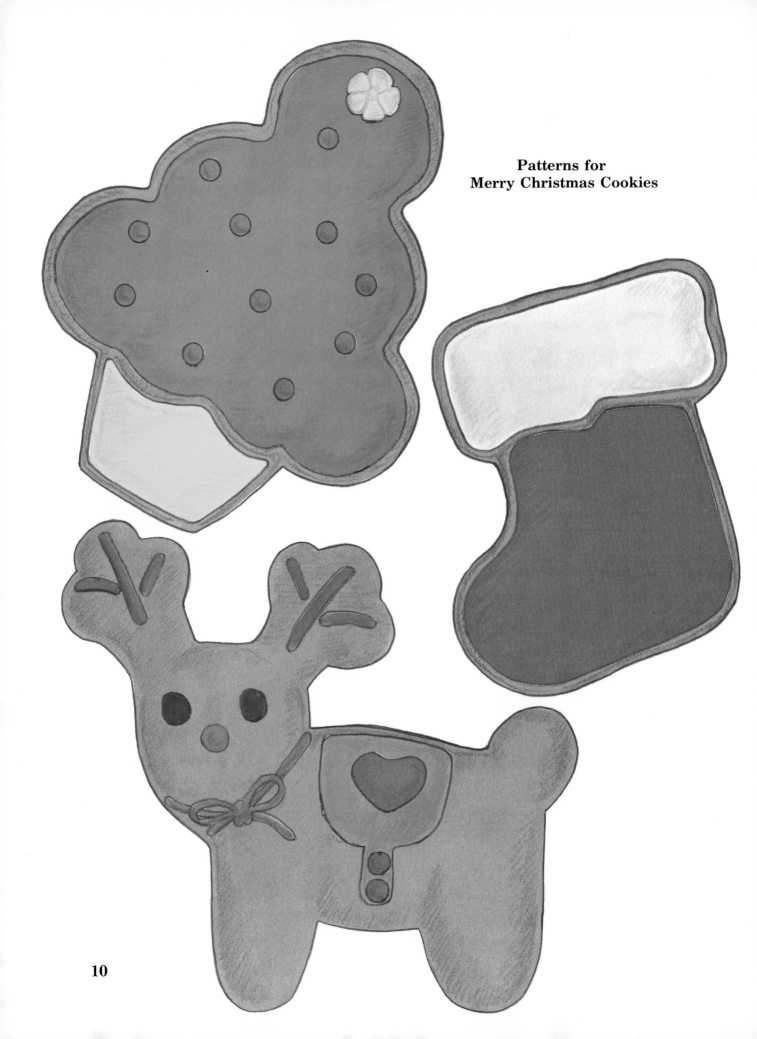

**Patterns for
Merry Christmas Cookies**

10

Chocolate Yum-Yums

1 (18.25-ounce) package devil's food
cake mix without pudding
½ cup vegetable oil
2 eggs, beaten
½ cup chopped pecans (if you like)
6 (1.65-ounce) milk chocolate bars,
broken into rectangles
candy sprinkles

1. Preheat the oven to 350°.

2. Combine the cake mix, oil, and eggs
in a large bowl. Stir well. Stir in the
pecans.

3. Using a teaspoon, drop the batter by
spoonfuls onto ungreased cookie sheets,
spacing the cookies about 2″ apart. Bake
for 10 minutes.

4. While the cookies are still warm, place
a chocolate rectangle on the top of each
cookie. Gently spread the chocolate.
Sprinkle the cookies with the candy
sprinkles.

5. Move the cookies to wire racks to cool.
Makes about 5 dozen cookies. Yum-yum.

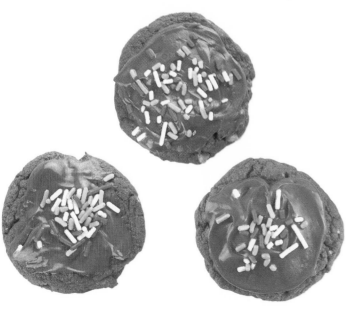

Peanut Butter Buttons

1 cup crunchy peanut butter
½ cup butter or margarine, softened
½ cup sugar
½ cup firmly packed brown sugar
½ teaspoon vanilla
1 egg
1½ cups sifted all-purpose flour
¾ teaspoon baking soda
½ teaspoon baking powder
¼ teaspoon salt
60 candy-coated chocolates

1. Preheat the oven to 350°.

2. In a large bowl, cream the peanut butter and butter. Add the white and brown
sugar, a little at a time, beating at medium speed of an electric mixer. Add the
vanilla and egg. Beat well.

3. Combine the flour, baking soda, baking powder, and salt. Sift together into
the peanut butter mixture. Mix well.

4. Shape the dough into 1″ balls. Place
the balls 2″ apart on ungreased cookie
sheets. Bake for 12 to 14 minutes or until
golden brown.

5. Top each cookie with a candy-coated
chocolate. Move the cookies to a wire rack
to cool. Makes 5 dozen cookies.

11

Cookie Quickies

Make these cookies with on-the-go sugar cookie dough—ready-made, refrigerated dough that you buy at the grocery store. To color the dough, put it in a heavy plastic food bag, add paste food coloring, and squeeze the bag to mix. Chill the dough in the freezer for about an hour before you slice, roll, or cut it. Bake the cookies in a preheated 350° oven, watching the first batch carefully to make sure the baking time is right for your oven.

Heart Cookies

1 package sugar cookie dough
red and green paste food coloring
flour for rolling the cookies
large heart, small heart, and round
  cookie cutters

1. Color half the dough red and the other half green.

2. Roll the chilled dough ⅛″ thick on a floured work surface. Cut hearts and rounds, using the cookie cutters. Put the little hearts on the big hearts and rounds.

3. Place the cookies on ungreased cookie sheets. Using a straw, make a hole in each cookie that you want to hang on your tree. Sprinkle the cookies with sugar, if you like.

4. Bake the cookies for 8 to 10 minutes. Let the cookies cool. Tie ribbons for hangers onto the cookies for the tree. Makes 1 to 2 dozen cookies, depending on the size.

Lollipop Cookies

1 package sugar cookie dough
30 lollipop sticks (about 4½″ long)
candy sprinkles

1. Slice the chilled dough into ¼″-thick slices and sprinkle with candy sprinkles.

2. On ungreased cookie sheets, place the first row of slices 2″ apart. Place the second row of slices about 5″ below the first row to allow room for the lollipop sticks.

3. Bake the cookies for 7 minutes and take the cookie sheets from the oven. Ask a grownup to push a lollipop stick into each cookie. Bake the cookies for about 3 more minutes. Let the cookies cool.

4. For presents, wrap each cookie in plastic wrap and tie a ribbon around the stick. Makes about 3 dozen cookies.

Holly Leaf Cookies

1 package sugar cookie dough
green paste food coloring
flour for rolling the cookies
red hots
holly leaf cookie cutter (small)

1. Color a third of the dough with the green food coloring.

2. Slice the chilled plain dough into ¼"-thick slices and place them on ungreased cookie sheets. Roll the chilled green dough ⅛" thick on a floured work surface. Cut out the leaves and place two on each cookie slice. Add red hots for berries.

3. Bake the cookies for 8 to 10 minutes. Let cool. Makes about 2 dozen cookies.

Snowman Cookies

1 package sugar cookie dough
green paste food coloring
red licorice, candy sprinkles, and
** silver candy balls**

1. Slice the chilled dough into ¼"-thick slices. Color several of the slices with the green food coloring. Place 18 of the slices on ungreased cookie sheets. From the remaining slices, roll 54 marble-sized balls for the snowmen. (If you have dough slices left over, you can make more snowman cookies or plain sugar cookies.)

2. For each cookie, place three balls on the cookie slice and press gently so that the balls touch. Using a damp Q-tip, place

candy sprinkles for the snowman's eyes, mouth, and buttons. Cut tiny pieces of red licorice for arms. Make a hat and a scarf with the green cookie dough. Top the hat with a silver candy ball.

3. Bake the cookies for 10 to 12 minutes. Let the cookies cool. Makes about 1½ dozen cookies.

Crushed Candy Cookies

1 package sugar cookie dough
4 rolls of small fruit-flavored candies

1. Separate the candies by color on a sheet of waxed paper. Place a sheet of waxed paper on top. Keeping the colors separate, coarsely crush the candies by tapping them gently with a hammer.

2. Slice the chilled dough into ¼"-thick slices. Using a small bottle cap, cut a hole in the center of each slice.

3. Line cookie sheets with aluminum foil. Place the cookie slices on the sheets and fill the holes with crushed candy.

4. Bake for 10 to 12 minutes. Let the cookies cool until the candy centers harden. Makes about 3 dozen cookies.

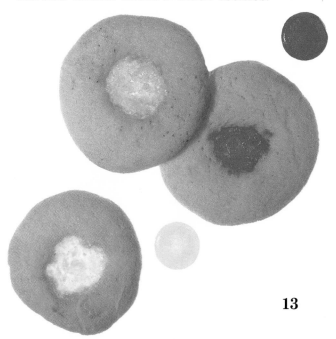

Fix tea for your teacher, caramel corn for cousins, or soup mix for the kind lady next door. Kitchen-made gifts are always special. How you wrap them can be, too!

December 87

Winter Warmers

To fix these instant drink mixes, put the ingredients in a plastic bag. Close with a bag tie—and shake!

Café au Lait

½ cup nondairy creamer
½ cup sugar
⅓ cup instant coffee powder

To serve: Place 1 tablespoon of mix in a cup. Add boiling water and stir.

Spiced Tea

1 (18-ounce) jar instant orange
　breakfast drink
1 (1-quart) package sweetened
　lemonade mix
2½ cups sugar
2 teaspoons cinnamon
¾ cup instant tea
½ teaspoon cloves

To serve: Place 2 to 3 heaping teaspoons of mix in a cup. Add boiling water and stir.

Hot Cocoa

2 cups nondairy creamer
1½ cups sugar
¾ cup unsweetened cocoa
½ cup nonfat dry milk
¼ teaspoon salt

To serve: Place 2 to 3 heaping teaspoons in a cup. Add boiling water and stir.

Snappy Wrap: Pick the animal wrap that you want to make. On a colored sack, draw a mouth. Cut out the mouth and cover the hole with plastic wrap. Use streamers for whiskers, stickers for eyes and nose, and poster paper cutouts for ears. Put a bag of drink mix in the sack. Fold the top of the sack toward the back and tape the edges. Attach a tag with serving directions.

15

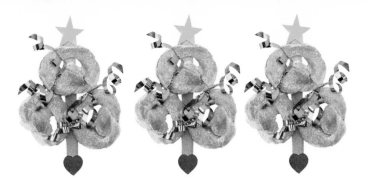

Pretzel Trees

1 package yeast
1½ cups warm water
1 teaspoon salt
1 tablespoon sugar
4 cups flour
1 egg, beaten
coarse salt
6 (6″-long) craft sticks
curling ribbon
heart and star stickers

1. Preheat the oven to 425°.

2. Dissolve the yeast in the warm water. Add the salt and sugar. Blend in the flour.

3. Sprinkle your work surface with flour and grease your hands. Knead the dough until smooth. Cut the dough into small pieces and roll the pieces into ropes that are ½″ across and 12″ long. Twist each rope into a pretzel shape.

4. Place one row of pretzels on a greased cookie sheet. Push a craft stick through every third pretzel and reshape the pretzel. Continue putting pretzels on the cookie sheet and inserting a craft stick in every third one.

5. Brush the pretzels with egg and sprinkle with coarse salt. Bake at 425° for 12 to 15 minutes. Let cool.

6. Using ribbon, tie a pretzel on each side of the pretzel on a stick. Stick a star sticker at the top of each stick and a heart sticker at the bottom. Makes six trees.

Caramel Corn

1 cup butter or margarine
½ cup light corn syrup
2 cups brown sugar
1 teaspoon salt
½ teaspoon baking soda
1 teaspoon vanilla
5 quarts popped corn

1. Preheat the oven to 250°.

2. Melt the butter in a large saucepan over low heat. Add the corn syrup, brown sugar, and salt. Stir to mix.

3. Bring the mixture to a boil over high heat. Boil for 5 minutes, stirring constantly. Remove the saucepan from the heat. Stir in the soda and vanilla.

4. Divide the popped corn into three 9″ x 13″ pans. Pour the cooked mixture over the popped corn and stir.

5. Bake for 1 hour. (Every 15 minutes, take the pans from the oven and stir the mixture, so that the popped corn will be evenly coated with caramel.)

6. Cover the countertop with waxed paper. Turn the caramel corn onto the waxed paper and let cool. Break into pieces. Store in covered containers.

Snappy Wrap: Glue colorful drawings, cutouts, and pieces of Christmas wrapping paper onto a box. Line the box with tissue paper and fill it with caramel corn.

Orange Butter

1 cup butter
2 tablespoons powdered sugar
grated rind of 1 lemon
grated rind of 1 orange
⅓ cup orange juice

1. Combine all the ingredients in a mixing bowl. Beat with an electric mixer until the orange juice is absorbed.

2. Store the butter in the refrigerator. Use as a spread on bread, biscuits, muffins, or pancakes. Makes 2 cups.

Buttermilk Biscuit Mix

4 cups all-purpose flour
2 tablespoons baking powder
1 teaspoon soda
¾ teaspoon salt
1 tablespoon sugar
⅔ cup shortening

1. Combine the flour, baking powder, soda, salt, and sugar in a large bowl. Mix well. Cut in the shortening.

2. Divide the mix into two 2-cup portions and place each portion in a plastic bag. Tie with a bag tie.

Snappy Wrap: Make a fabric bag, following the instructions on page 53. Place a 2-cup bag of mix inside the fabric bag.

Make a recipe card. Write the directions for Buttermilk Biscuits on the card and attach it to the bag.

Buttermilk Biscuits

Add 1 cup of buttermilk to the biscuit mix and stir to mix. Using a tablespoon, drop the dough by spoonfuls onto a lightly greased baking sheet. Bake in a 450° oven for 10 minutes or until golden brown. Makes about 8 biscuits.

Bouquet Garni

1 tablespoon dried parsley flakes
1 teaspoon dried whole thyme
¼ teaspoon dried whole rosemary
4 whole peppercorns
1 bay leaf

1. Place all the ingredients in the center of a square of cheesecloth. Gather up the corners of the cheesecloth and tie tightly with a piece of cotton twine.

2. Store in a covered container. Use for seasoning soups, stocks, and sauces. Makes 1 bouquet garni.

Snappy Wrap: Make a poster paper wreath and glue a bow at the top. For each bouquet garni, punch two holes, side by side, in the wreath. Pull a ribbon through the holes. Wrap the bouquets garnis in colorful fabric squares and tie them to the wreath with the ribbons.

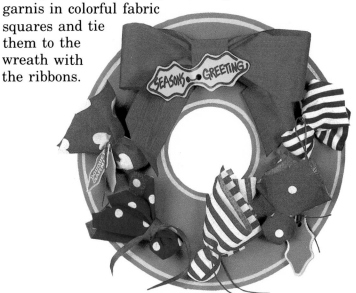

Nine Bean Soup Mix

1 pound barley pearls
1 pound dried black beans
1 pound dried red beans
1 pound dried pinto beans
1 pound dried navy beans
1 pound dried Great Northern beans
1 pound dried lentils
1 pound dried green split peas
1 pound dried black-eyed peas

1. Combine and mix all of the beans in a very big bowl.

2. Put 2 cups of beans in each of 10 plastic bags. Close with bag ties.

Snappy Wrap: Using the patterns on page 49 as a guide, draw a big bear on heavy cardboard. Cut out the bear. Punch two holes under the bear's chin. Pull a ribbon through the holes and tie it around a bag of beans. Decorate with heart stickers. Draw and cut out a big heart. Write the recipe for Nine Bean Soup on the heart and tape it to the bear.

Nine Bean Soup

2 cups Nine Bean Soup Mix
2 quarts water
1 pound ham, diced
1 large onion, chopped
1 clove garlic, minced
½ to ¾ teaspoon salt
1 (16-ounce) can tomatoes, undrained and chopped
1 (10-ounce) can tomatoes and green chilies, undrained

Sort and wash the bean mix; place in a Dutch oven. Cover with water 2″ above beans, and soak overnight. Drain beans; add 2 quarts water and next 4 ingredients. Cover and bring to a boil; reduce heat, and simmer 1½ hours or until beans are tender. Add remaining ingredients; simmer 30 minutes, stirring occasionally. Makes 8 cups.

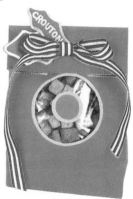

Easy Cheesy Croutons

1 tablespoon butter
2 tablespoons grated Parmesan cheese
2 cups bread cubes

1. Preheat the oven to 350°.

2. Melt the butter in a saucepan over low heat. Mix the butter and cheese in a bowl. Add the bread cubes and toss.

3. Spread the bread cubes on a baking sheet and bake until golden brown. Store in a closed bag or covered container.

Snappy Wrap: On a colored sack, draw a circle and cut it out. From this circle, cut a smaller circle. Tape a piece of plastic wrap over the hole and glue the small circle to the outside. Put a bag of croutons in the sack. Fold down the top, punch two holes, and pull a ribbon through the holes. Make a gift tag. Punch a hole in the tag and attach it with the ribbon.

Sundae Sauce

1 (6-ounce) package milk chocolate
  morsels
¼ cup crunchy peanut butter
¼ cup light corn syrup
¼ cup plus 1 tablespoon whipping
  cream

1. Melt the chocolate morsels in the top
of a double boiler. Add the peanut butter
and mix well.

2. Take the mixture off the stove. Stir in
the corn syrup and whipping cream.

3. Store the sauce in a covered container
in the refrigerator. Reheat over low heat
before using. Makes about 1¼ cups.

Snappy Wrap: Put the sauce in a jar
and screw on the lid. Put several squares
of tissue paper over the lid and hold them
in place with a rubber band. Draw, color,
and cut out a sundae tag. Tie a ribbon
around the lid and attach the tag.

Heavenly Mints

1 (16-ounce) package powdered sugar
½ cup margarine, softened
2 tablespoons evaporated milk
4 to 5 drops of peppermint flavoring
2 to 3 drops of food coloring

1. Combine all of the ingredients in a
large mixing bowl. Beat at high speed of
an electric mixer until well blended.

2. Knead the mixture until smooth.

3. Cover cookie sheets with paper towels.
Shape the mixture in rubber candy molds.
Put the shapes on the cookie sheets and
cover with paper towels.

4. Let the mints stand overnight to
harden. Store in covered containers, placing waxed paper between layers. Makes 8
to 9 dozen mints.

Snappy Wrap: Using the pattern on
page 55, draw angels on stiff paper and
cut them out. Punch two holes in the center of each angel and pull a ribbon
through the holes. Wrap the mints in
squares of plastic wrap. Tie the mints to
the angels.

CHILDREN'S WORKSHOP

Happy Holiday Crafts

Sugar 'n Spice

These trimmings are quick and easy to make. What a sweet touch they'll add to your tree!

Gingerbread Folks

You will need:
pencil
tracing paper
scissors
medium-grade sandpaper
cinnamon stick
measuring spoons
powdered white tempera paint
white glue
bowl
squeeze bottle
hole punch
yarn

Candy Canes

You will need:
pencil
tracing paper
scissors
white poster paper
pinking shears
white glue
36″ piece of thick red yarn
fishing line

Gingerbread Man

1. Trace and cut out the pattern for the gingerbread man. On the back of the sandpaper, draw around the pattern. Cut out the gingerbread man.

2. To make the gingerbread man smell spicy, rub the sandy side with the cinnamon stick.

3. Mix two teaspoons of paint with four tablespoons of glue in the bowl. Spoon the mixture into the squeeze bottle.

4. Squeeze some of the glue mixture onto a scrap of sandpaper. If the mixture is too thick, add more glue. If the mixture is too thin, add more paint.

5. Draw features on the gingerbread man with the glue mixture. Let the glue mixture dry.

6. Punch a hole in the gingerbread man's head with the hole punch. For a hanger, cut a piece of yarn and pull it through the hole. Tie a bow with the ends of the yarn.

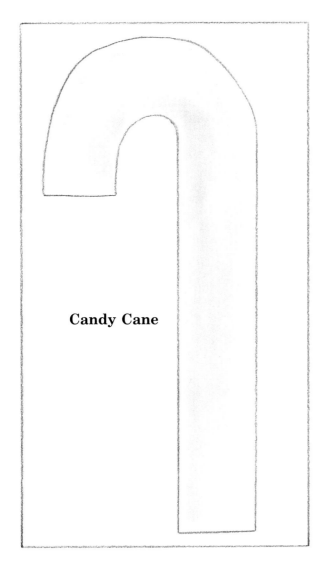

Candy Cane

1. Trace the pattern for the candy cane on tracing paper. Cut out the candy cane with scissors.

2. Draw around the candy cane on poster paper. Using pinking shears, cut out the poster paper cane.

3. On the back of the candy cane, glue one end of the yarn at the bottom. Let the glue dry. Wrap the yarn around the candy cane to make stripes. Glue the loose end of the yarn to the back of the candy cane. Let the glue dry.

4. Poke a hole in the top of the candy cane. To make a hanger, pull a piece of fishing line through the hole and tie a knot with the ends.

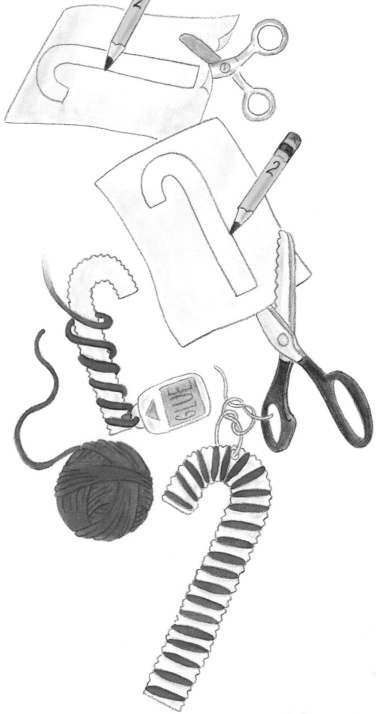

Frosty Flakes

No snow? Make your own bright white flakes. Invite a buddy to share in the fun.

For safety's sake: Be sure to follow the directions on the back of the can of spray snow. Ask a grown-up to read these with you and to help if you need it.

You will need:
newspaper
round toothpicks
white glue
1″ plastic foam ball
ornament hanger
white acrylic paint
paintbrush
can of spray snow

1. Spread newspaper over your work area.

2. Put a drop of glue on one end of each toothpick and stick the toothpicks in the plastic foam ball.

3. Push the ornament hanger into the top of the ball.

4. Paint the toothpicks and ball. Let the paint dry.

5. Lightly spray the snowflake with snow. Let dry. Spray the snowflake again. Let the snow dry.

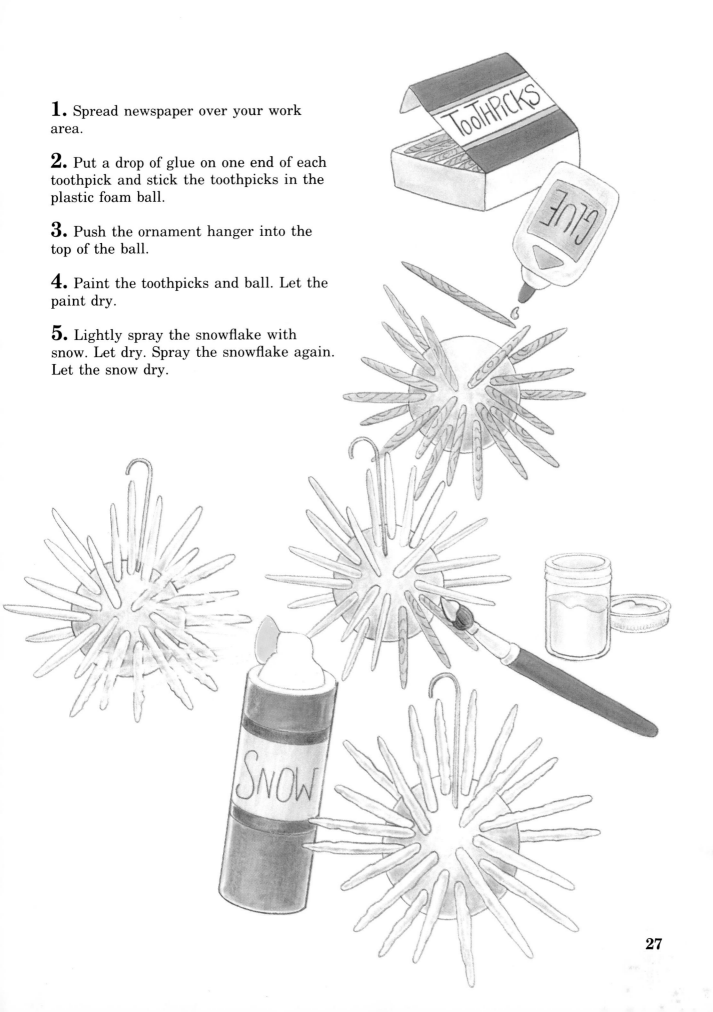

Hobby the Horse

Oh, how happy Hobby will be, rocking around your Christmas tree!

You will need:
pencil
tracing paper
scissors
Tacky Glue
two 6″ squares of felt
two 6″ squares of poster paper
nail (for poking holes)
ruler
yarn
felt for ears and saddle
large paper clip
gold thread
sequins

1. Trace the patterns for the horse, ear, and saddle on tracing paper. Cut out the patterns.

2. Glue the 6″ squares of felt to the 6″ squares of poster paper. Let the glue dry.

3. On the paper side of one square, draw around the horse pattern. Turn the horse pattern over and draw around it on the paper side of the other square. Cut out the horses.

4. Using the nail and looking at the pattern to see where the holes should be, poke holes in the horses. Place the horses with the paper sides together.

5. For the mane, cut one 5″ piece and four 3″ pieces of yarn. Pull the 5″ piece of yarn through the head holes and tie it around the other pieces of yarn. (If you have trouble pulling the yarn through the holes, wrap a piece of tape around one end of the yarn. Pull the end through the holes and cut off the tape.) Cut a few short pieces of yarn and glue these between the foreheads for "bangs."

6. For the tail, cut nine 5″ pieces of yarn. Pull one piece of yarn through the holes and tie it around the other eight pieces.

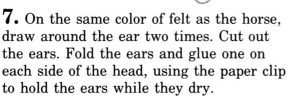

7. On the same color of felt as the horse, draw around the ear two times. Cut out the ears. Fold the ears and glue one on each side of the head, using the paper clip to hold the ears while they dry.

8. On a different color of felt, draw around the saddle. Cut out the saddle and glue one side of it to one side of the horse. Cut a piece of gold thread for a hanger and run it under the middle of the saddle. Glue the other side of the saddle to the other side of the horse. Tie the ends of the thread.

9. Glue sequins on the saddle. Glue a sequin eye on each side of the horse. Let the glue dry.

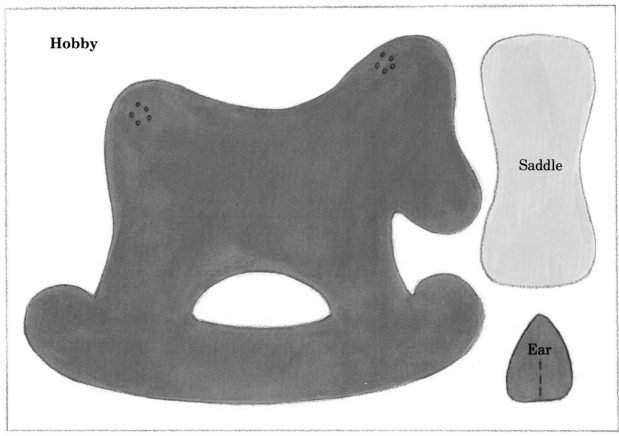

Hobby

Saddle

Ear

Pom-Pom Wreaths

Pom-pom wreaths are pretty. Hang some on your tree. Give others for presents.

You will need:
white glue
package of green pom-poms
wooden drapery ring
package of tiny red pom-poms
narrow ribbon
red embroidery floss (or string)

1. Squeeze a little bit of glue onto a green pom-pom. Glue the pom-pom to the drapery ring. Keep gluing green pom-poms around the ring until the ring looks like a wreath.

2. For berries, glue tiny red pom-poms onto the wreath. Let the glue dry.

3. Pull a ribbon through the hook on the ring. Tie the ribbon into a bow.

4. To make a hanger, cut a piece of embroidery floss and pull it through the hook. Tie a knot with the ends of the floss.

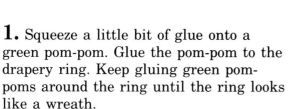

Holiday Houses

Make a townful of these little houses. Trim them with fabric scraps, ribbon, and lace.

For safety's sake: Let a grown-up do the cutting with the sharp knife.

You will need:
pencil
tracing paper
carbon paper
4″ square of 1″-thick plastic foam
ruler
sharp knife
dinner knife
scissors
pins with colored heads
scraps of fabric
Tacky Glue
felt in same colors as fabric scraps
scraps of lace
cotton ball
ribbon (for trim and hanger)

Cutting Out the House

1. Trace the pattern for the house on tracing paper.

2. Place the piece of carbon paper face down on the piece of plastic foam and put the pattern on top. Using the pencil and ruler, trace the pattern onto the plastic foam.

3. Ask a grown-up to cut along the outline of the house with the sharp knife. Using the dinner knife, make grooves about ¼″ deep along the lines inside the outline.

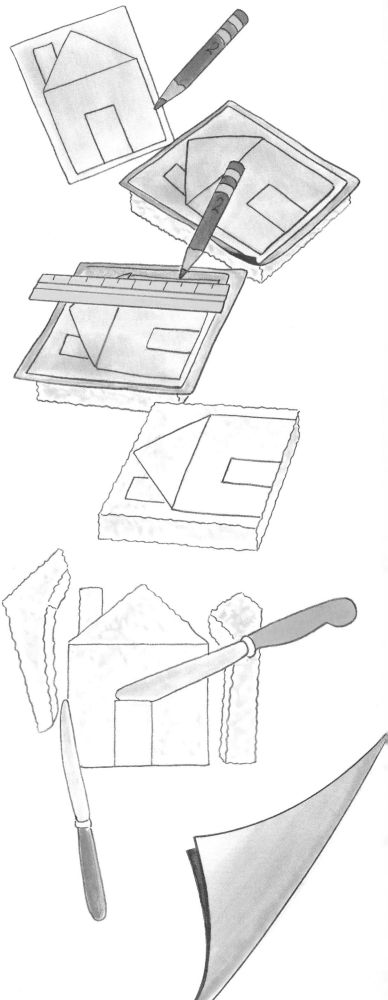

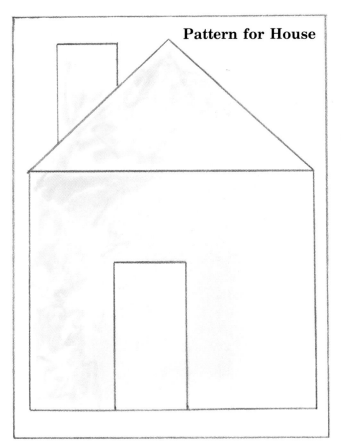

Pattern for House

Decorating the House

1. Trace the patterns for the fabric pieces. Cut out the patterns and pin them to the fabric scraps. Cut out the fabric pieces. On the house front, cut slits above the door as marked.

2. Center the fabric roof over the roof on the plastic foam house. Use the dinner knife to tuck the fabric edges that run along the grooves into the grooves. Wrap the other fabric edges toward the back of the house and glue them in place. (You may want to trim these edges before gluing them.) Use pins to hold the roof edges while the glue dries.

3. Attach the house front, chimney, and door to the house in the same way as the roof.

4. Cut a 1″ x 14½″ strip of felt. Glue the strip around the roof, sides, and bottom of the house. Let the glue dry.

5. Draw around the house on a piece of felt. Cut out the felt house and glue it to the back of the plastic foam house. Let the glue dry.

6. Glue or pin pieces of fabric, lace, and ribbon onto the house for trim. Use a pin for the doorknob. Pull a cotton ball apart and glue it to the chimney for smoke. Let the glue dry.

7. To make a hanger, cut a piece of ribbon. Pin the ends of the ribbon to the back of the house at the peak of the roof.

34

Patterns for Fabric Pieces

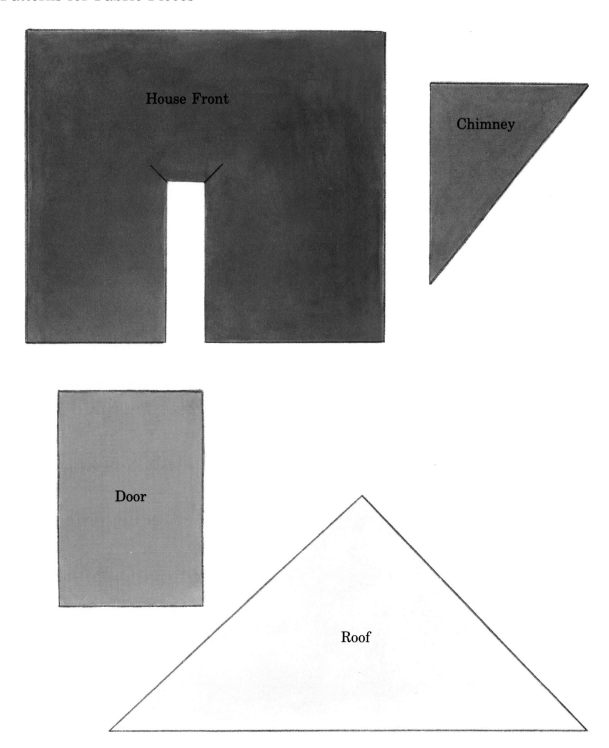

Countdown Santa

Ho, ho, ho! Mark the days before Christmas on this special calendar. Watch Santa's beard grow fluffy and full.

You will need:
pencil
tracing paper
scissors
felt (red, white, pink, green, and black)
16″ square of white poster paper
black felt-tip marker
glue stick
1 large red pom-pom
12″ piece of narrow green ribbon
hole punch
red felt-tip marker
25 large white pom-poms (or cotton balls)

1. Trace and cut out the patterns.

2. Draw around the hat on red felt, the hat ball and brim on white felt, and the face on pink felt. Draw around the holly leaf two times on green felt. Cut out the felt pieces.

3. Place the pattern for Santa's beard at the bottom of the poster paper. Draw around the beard with the black marker.

4. Glue Santa's face at the top of the beard. Glue the hat brim, hat, and hat ball in place. Let the glue dry.

5. Cut out Santa, cutting along the outline of the beard and hat.

6. Cut two black felt circles for eyes and glue them in place. Glue on the red pompom for a nose. Glue the ribbon across the top of the hat brim. Use the hole punch to make red felt berries. Glue the holly leaves and berries in place. Let the glue dry.

7. Using the pencil, lightly write the numbers 1 through 25 on Santa's beard. Trace the numbers with the red marker. Beginning on December 1, glue one pompom a day onto Santa's beard.

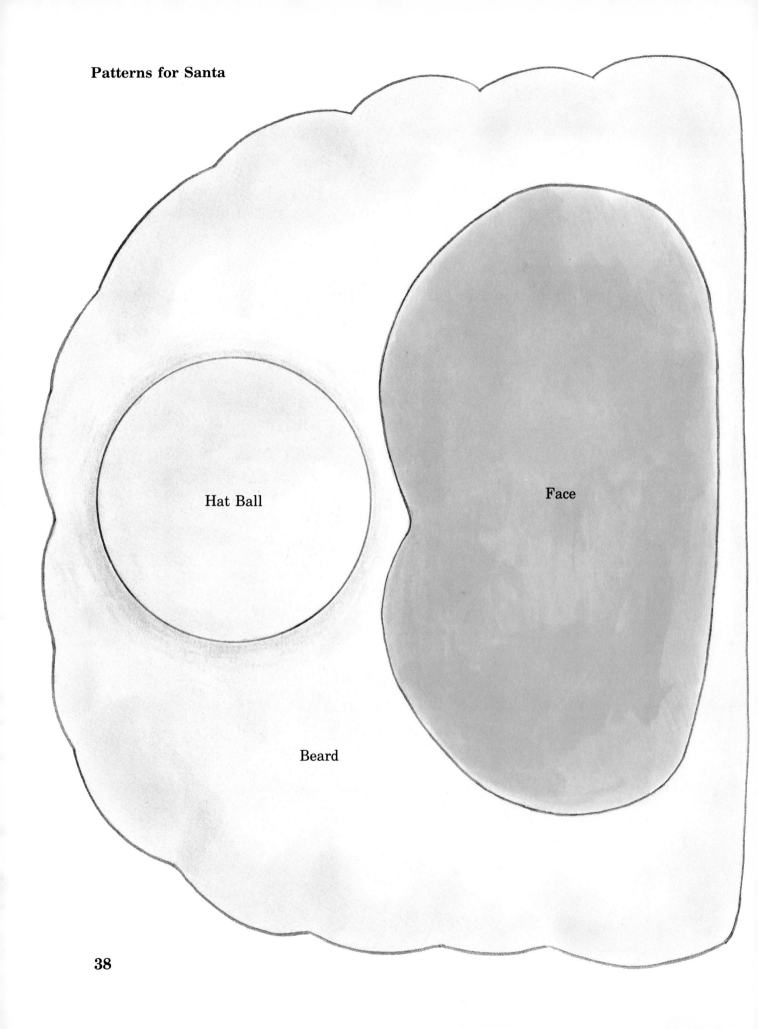

Hat Ball

Face

Beard

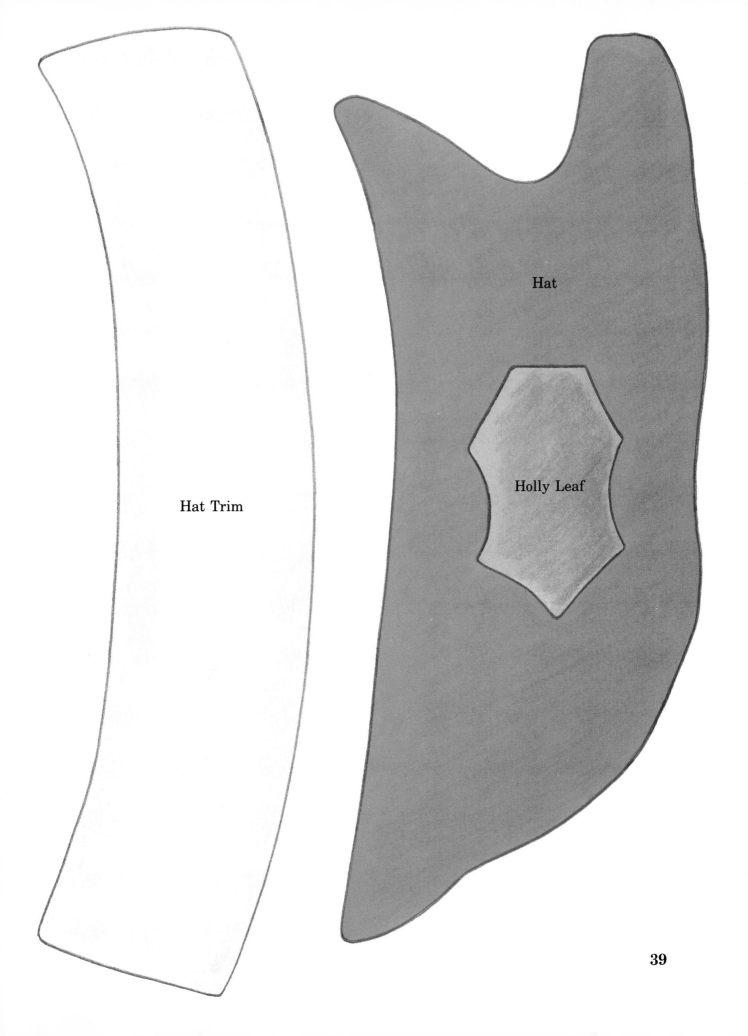

Hat Trim

Hat

Holly Leaf

39

Paper Candles

How pretty these candles will look in a window. Blow on the flames. See how they flicker!

You will need:
scissors
paper towel roll
wrapping paper
clear tape
pencil
tracing paper
red and green construction paper
yellow poster paper
white glue
6″ piece of fishing line

1. Cut the paper towel roll to the height that you want your candle to be.

2. Cut a piece of wrapping paper that is big enough to wrap the paper towel roll. Wrap the roll, turning the top and bottom edges of the paper to the inside of the roll. Tape the side edge of the paper.

3. Trace and cut out the patterns for the candle flame and glow circle. Draw around the candle flame two times on red paper and the glow circle two times on yellow paper. Cut out the paper pieces.

4. Glue the middle of the fishing line between the flames. Center the flames between the glow circles. Glue the glow circles together. Let the glue dry. Cut off the ends of the fishing line.

5. Trace and cut out the pattern for the candle holder. Fold the piece of green paper and place the pattern on it as marked. Draw around the pattern. Cut out the candle holder. Cut the slits.

6. Unfold the candle holder and turn it over. Fold side B up 1½″. Lap side A over the 1½″ strip and tape the two together. Lap side C over side D and tape.

7. At the top of the candle, cut a 1″ slit down one side. Cut another 1″ slit down the opposite side. Slide the glow circle and flame into the slits. Place the candle in the holder.

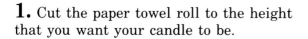

**Patterns for
Paper Candles**

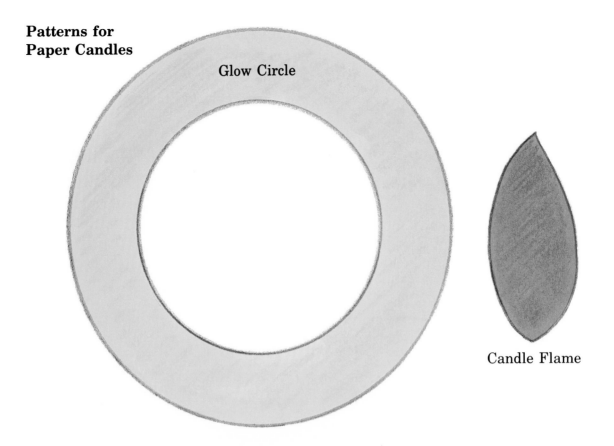

Glow Circle

Candle Flame

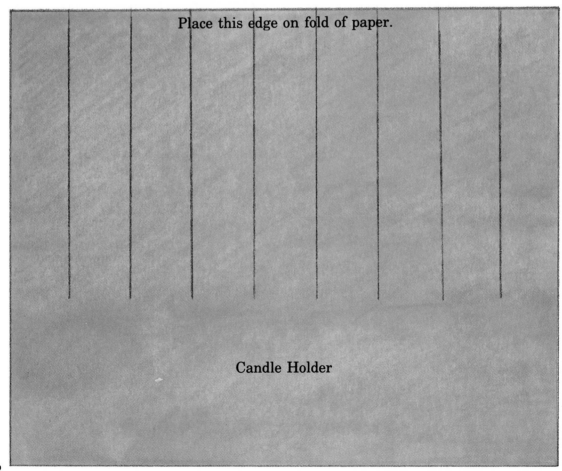

Place this edge on fold of paper.

Candle Holder

Holly Leaf Wreath

Surprise your teacher with a "holly-day" wreath. Ask your class to help draw and cut out the leaves.

You will need:
pencil
pizza pan (about 13″ across)
green paper (heavy weight)
scissors
salad plate (about 8″ across)
tracing paper
white glue
paper clips
thin wire (for attaching bow)
ribbon bow

1. Draw around the pizza pan on the green paper. Cut out the circle.

2. Place the salad plate in the center of the circle. Draw around the plate. Cut out the small circle to make a wreath.

3. Trace and cut out the holly leaf. Draw around it 18 times on the green paper. Cut out the leaves and fold them in half. Crease the folds. Unfold the leaves.

4. Glue the leaves around the wreath. Use paper clips to hold the leaves in place while the glue dries.

5. Pull the wire through the back of the bowknot. Poke two holes in the wreath and pull the ends of the wire through the holes. Twist the ends together.

Angel Fun

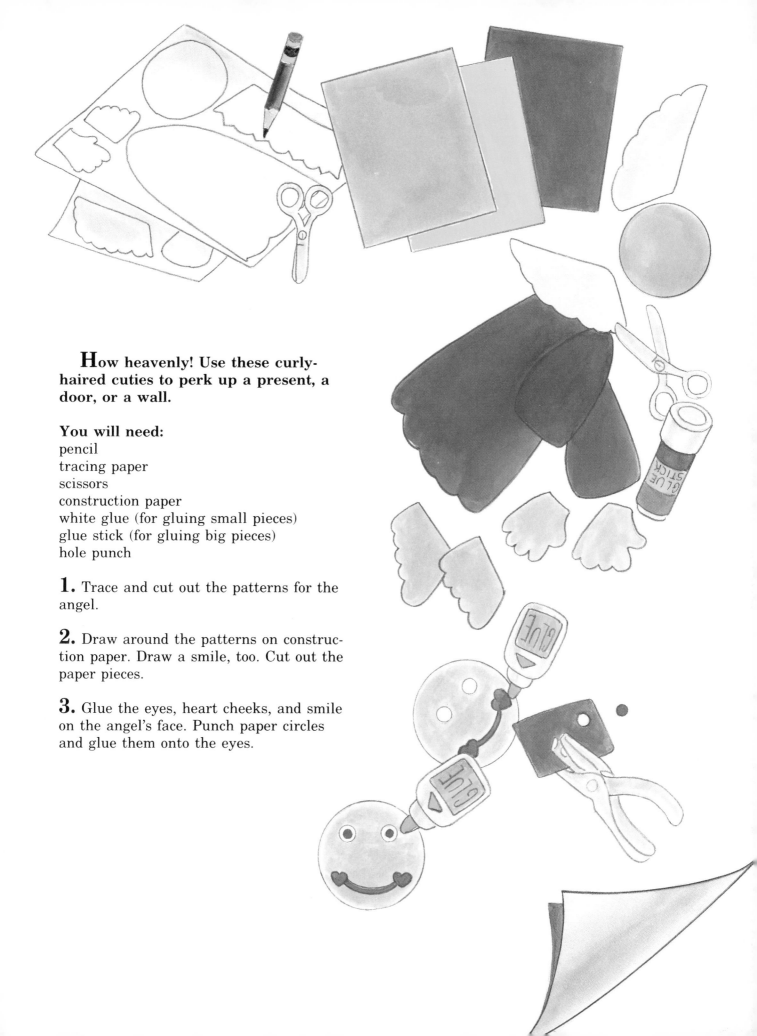

How heavenly! Use these curly-haired cuties to perk up a present, a door, or a wall.

You will need:
pencil
tracing paper
scissors
construction paper
white glue (for gluing small pieces)
glue stick (for gluing big pieces)
hole punch

1. Trace and cut out the patterns for the angel.

2. Draw around the patterns on construction paper. Draw a smile, too. Cut out the paper pieces.

3. Glue the eyes, heart cheeks, and smile on the angel's face. Punch paper circles and glue them onto the eyes.

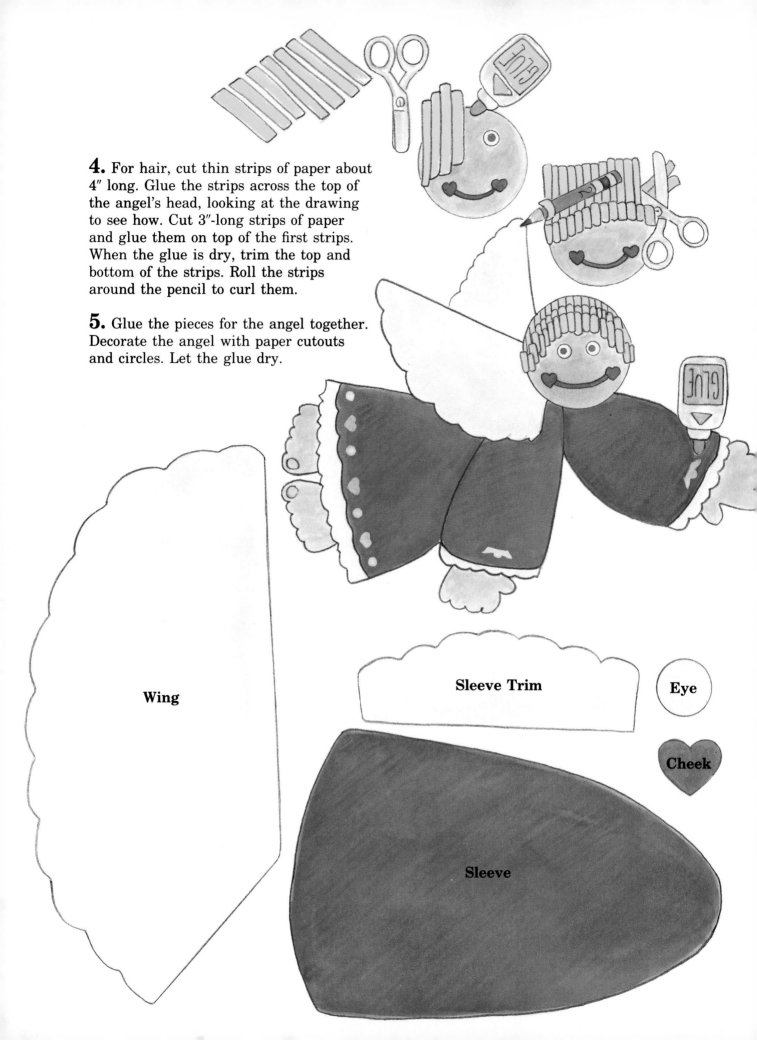

4. For hair, cut thin strips of paper about 4″ long. Glue the strips across the top of the angel's head, looking at the drawing to see how. Cut 3″-long strips of paper and glue them on top of the first strips. When the glue is dry, trim the top and bottom of the strips. Roll the strips around the pencil to curl them.

5. Glue the pieces for the angel together. Decorate the angel with paper cutouts and circles. Let the glue dry.

Wing

Sleeve Trim

Eye

Cheek

Sleeve

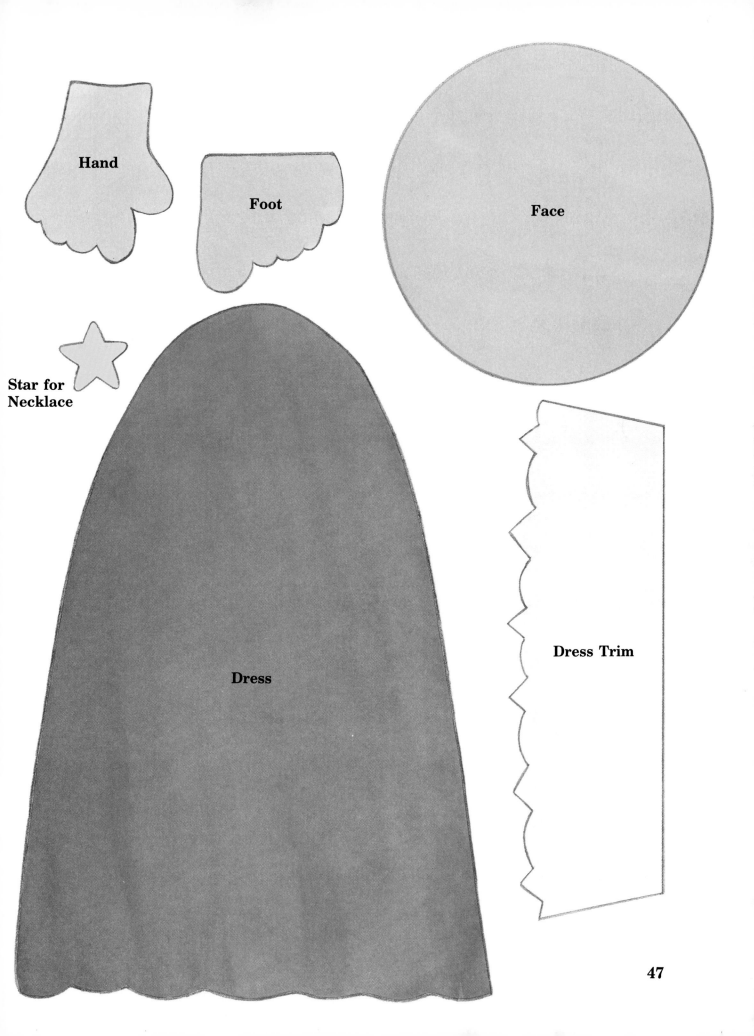

Hand

Foot

Face

Star for
Necklace

Dress

Dress Trim

47

Chummy Bears

Turned upside down or right side up, these tags look "bear-y" nice on presents!

You will need:
pencil
tracing paper
carbon paper
grocery sack
fine-tip markers
colored pencils
scissors
ribbon
white glue
scraps of white and colored wrapping paper
white poster paper
wrapped packages

1. Trace the patterns for the bears. Place the carbon paper face down on the grocery sack and put the tracing of the bears on top. Using the pencil, trace the patterns onto the sack.

2. Use the markers and colored pencils to outline and color the bears.

3. Cut out the bears. Cut slits along the paws, looking at the pattern for the big bear to see where to make the slits.

4. Cut pieces of ribbon and tie them into bows. Glue the bows onto the bears' necks. Let the glue dry.

5. To make gift tags, glue small pieces of white wrapping paper to bigger pieces of colored wrapping paper. When the glue is dry, write your messages.

6. Trace and cut out the patterns for the candy canes. Draw around the candy canes on poster paper. Cut out the poster-paper candy canes. Color stripes on them with a red marker.

7. Attach each bear by slipping its back paws over a ribbon on a wrapped package, or by gluing it to the package. Tuck a candy cane in one front paw. Push a ribbon through the other front paw. Glue the ends of the ribbon to a gift tag. Let the glue dry.

Cut. Cut.

Cut.

Manger Card

And she . . . wrapped Him in swaddling cloths, and laid Him in a manger, because there was no place for them in the inn.

Luke 2:7

In a manger filled with straw, Baby Jesus reminds us of that very first Christmas.

You will need:
construction paper
scissors
pencil
tracing paper
white poster paper
scrap of unbleached muslin
white glue
pink and black fine-tip markers
gold glitter
packing straw

1. Fold a piece of construction paper with the ends together. Cut along the fold line. Fold each paper half from side to side to make a card.

2. Trace and cut out the patterns for the Baby Jesus, manger, star, and halo.

3. Draw around Baby Jesus' body on poster paper. Draw around the manger, star, halo, and Baby Jesus' face on construction paper. Cut out the paper pieces.

4. Tear the muslin into ½″-wide strips. Spread glue over Baby Jesus' body and wrap the strips around it. Glue the strips to hold them in place.

5. Glue Baby Jesus' face to the body. Use the markers to draw the features.

6. Spread the star and halo with glue and sprinkle them with glitter. Let the glue dry. Shake off the glitter that did not stick.

7. Glue the manger, Baby Jesus, star, and halo onto the card. Glue straw along the top of the manger. Let the glue dry.

Patterns for Manger Card

Sew-Easy Bags

Plain or fancy, fabric bags are perfect for holding gifts like seed for Grandma's birds and popcorn for friends. If you've never sewn with a machine before, ask a grown-up for help. Once you've stitched the first bag, the rest will be easy.

For safety's sake: Be careful with the iron.

You will need:
sewing scissors
fabrics in Christmas colors
sewing machine
tape measure
iron
straight pins
⅞″-wide ribbon
safety pin
pencil
piece of clear, heavy-weight plastic
masking tape
butcher paper (or newsprint)
acrylic paint
aluminum pie pan
paintbrush with stiff bristles

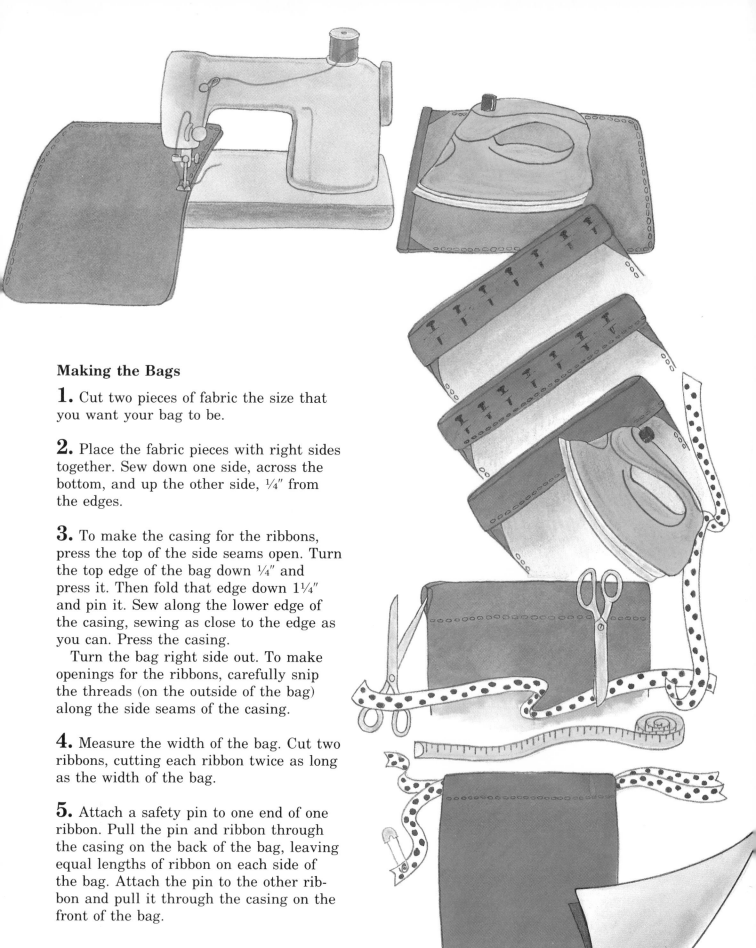

Making the Bags

1. Cut two pieces of fabric the size that you want your bag to be.

2. Place the fabric pieces with right sides together. Sew down one side, across the bottom, and up the other side, ¼″ from the edges.

3. To make the casing for the ribbons, press the top of the side seams open. Turn the top edge of the bag down ¼″ and press it. Then fold that edge down 1¼″ and pin it. Sew along the lower edge of the casing, sewing as close to the edge as you can. Press the casing.

Turn the bag right side out. To make openings for the ribbons, carefully snip the threads (on the outside of the bag) along the side seams of the casing.

4. Measure the width of the bag. Cut two ribbons, cutting each ribbon twice as long as the width of the bag.

5. Attach a safety pin to one end of one ribbon. Pull the pin and ribbon through the casing on the back of the bag, leaving equal lengths of ribbon on each side of the bag. Attach the pin to the other ribbon and pull it through the casing on the front of the bag.

Stenciling the Bags

1. To make a stencil, trace the pattern for the tree, holly leaf, or angel on the piece of clear plastic. Cut into one side of the plastic and cut out the pattern. Tape the cut edge of the plastic back together.

2. Cover your worktable with a piece of butcher paper. Cut a piece of butcher paper the size of your bag. Place the paper inside the bag. (When you stencil, the paper will absorb the paint and keep it off the back of the bag.)

3. Decide where you want your stenciled design to be. Place the stencil on top of the bag. Put little pieces of tape around the edges of the stencil to hold it in place.

4. Put some paint in the pie pan. Dab the paintbrush in the paint. (A fairly dry brush works best, so don't get the brush dripping wet.) Dab the brush up and down inside the cutout shape in the stencil. Keep dabbing on paint until the design is complete. Take the stencil off the bag.

5. Stencil the design as many times as you like. To make berries around the holly leaf, dip a pencil eraser into red paint and stamp the bag. Let the paint dry. Remove the paper from inside the bag.

6. Put a present inside the bag. (If the present is something to eat, first put it in a plastic bag.) Hold the ribbon ends and gather the top of the bag to close it. Tie the ribbon ends on each side of the bag into a bow.

Stencil Patterns

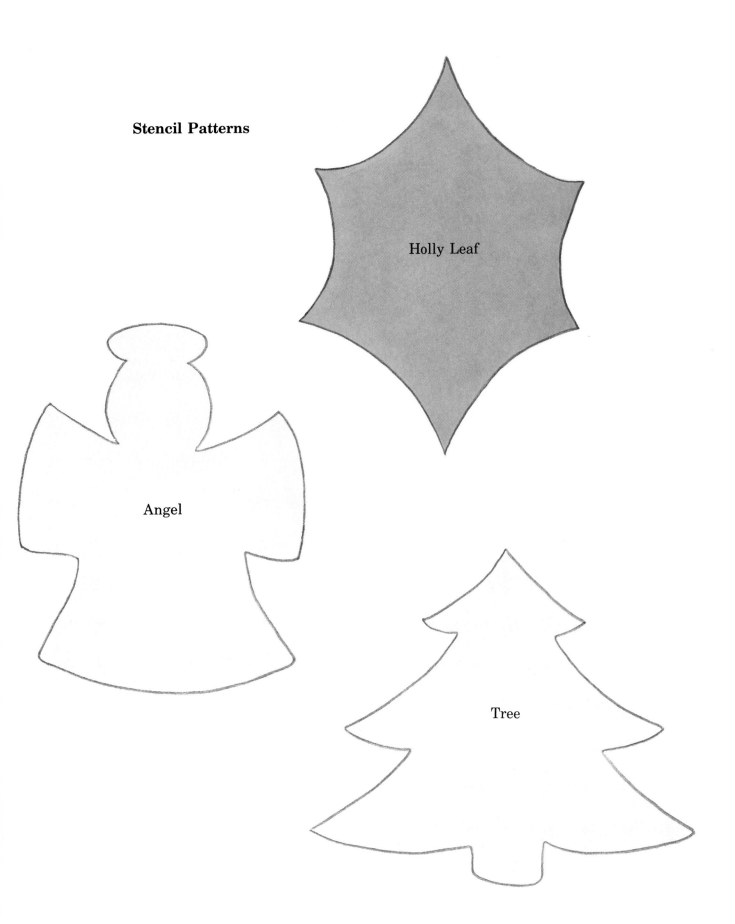

Holly Leaf

Angel

Tree

Snow Show

Do you know what to do with these? Just shake them. Wow! Look at that snow!

Before you start: Fill the baby food jar with tap water, screw on the lid, and turn the jar upside down. Let it sit awhile to make sure that it does not leak. If it does, try another lid.

You will need:
baby food jar and lid (clean and dry)
red acrylic paint
paintbrush
Elmer's Stix-All (or other water-resistant glue)
small Christmas ornament
small piece of polyester stuffing
tablespoon
white glitter
distilled water
16″ piece of narrow ribbon

1. Paint the lid red, applying two or three coats of paint and letting the paint dry between coats.

2. When the last coat of paint is dry, glue the bottom of the ornament to the inside of the lid. Let the glue set.

3. Pull the piece of stuffing apart. Make a circle of glue on the lid around the ornament. Put a little stuffing for snow along the circle of glue. Let the glue dry.

4. Put a tablespoon of glitter in the jar. Pour enough distilled water in the jar to almost fill it.

5. Carefully place the lid on the jar and screw the lid tight.

6. Turn the jar upside down. Tie the ribbon around the lid and make a bow.

Fancy Frames

Give your mom a colorful frame. Put a picture of someone special— like yourself—inside.

You will need:
pencil
ruler
white poster paper
scissors
white glue
waxed paper
gesso
paintbrushes
paper towels
acrylic paints
tracing paper
wrapping paper (to match paint colors)
clear tape
ribbon bow

Making the Frame

1. For each frame, measure and cut two 6½″ x 8″ pieces of poster paper.

2. Measure and mark 1½″ from the edges of each piece. Using your ruler as a guide, draw lines through the marks to make rectangles. Cut out the rectangles, and you'll have two frames.

3. To make one thick frame, glue the two frames together. Wrap the frame in waxed paper and put it under some books until the glue is dry.

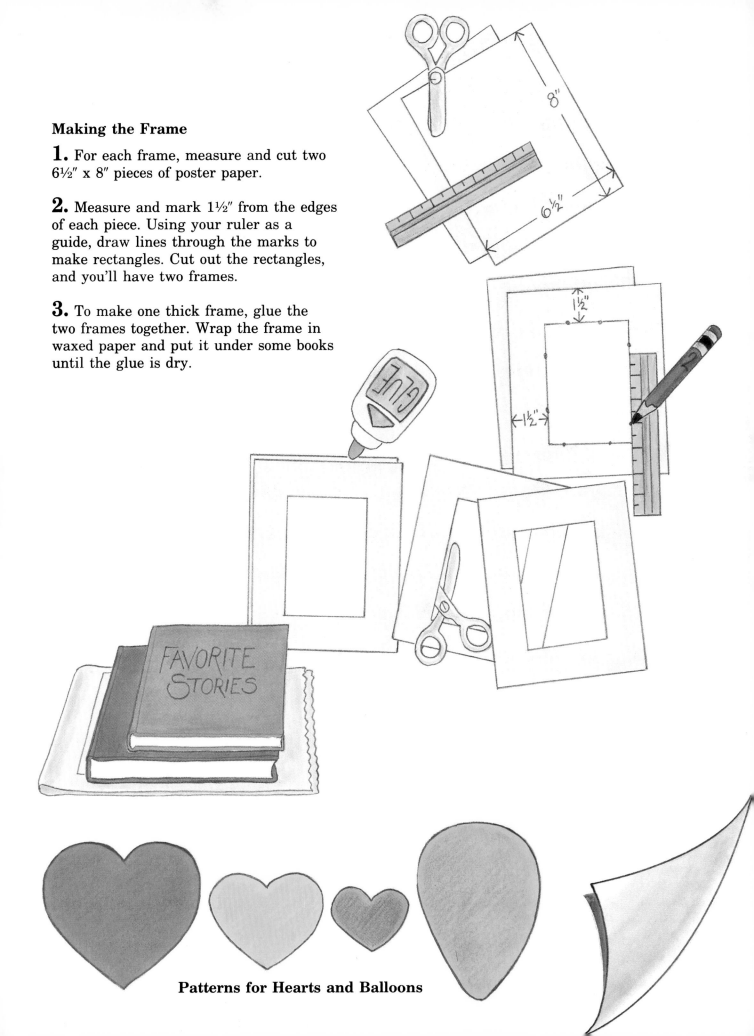

Patterns for Hearts and Balloons

Painting the Frame

1. Paint the front of the frame with gesso. Rinse your brush in water and wipe it with a paper towel. (Remember to rinse and wipe your brush each time you are finished with the gesso or want to change the color of your paint.) Let the gesso dry.

2. Use the pencil and ruler to draw a border around the frame opening. Paint the border and let dry.

3. Paint the front of the frame. When the paint is dry, paint the outer edges of the back of the frame. Let the paint dry.

4. For the Happy Hearts Frame, trace and cut out the patterns for the hearts. Draw around the patterns on poster paper. Cut out the poster paper hearts. Paint the hearts and let dry.

5. For the Bubbly Balloons Frame, trace and cut out the pattern for the balloon. Draw around the balloon six times on poster paper. Cut out the balloons and glue them together in twos. Brush the balloons with gesso and let dry. Paint the balloons. Let the paint dry.

6. Glue the hearts or balloons to the frame. Paint strings if you're making the balloons frame. Let dry.

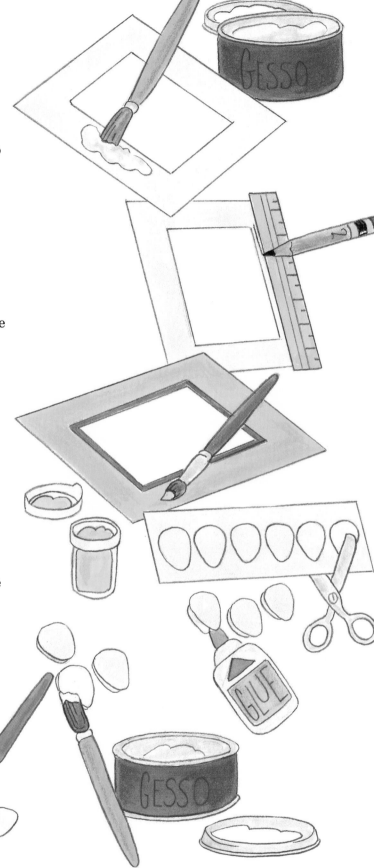

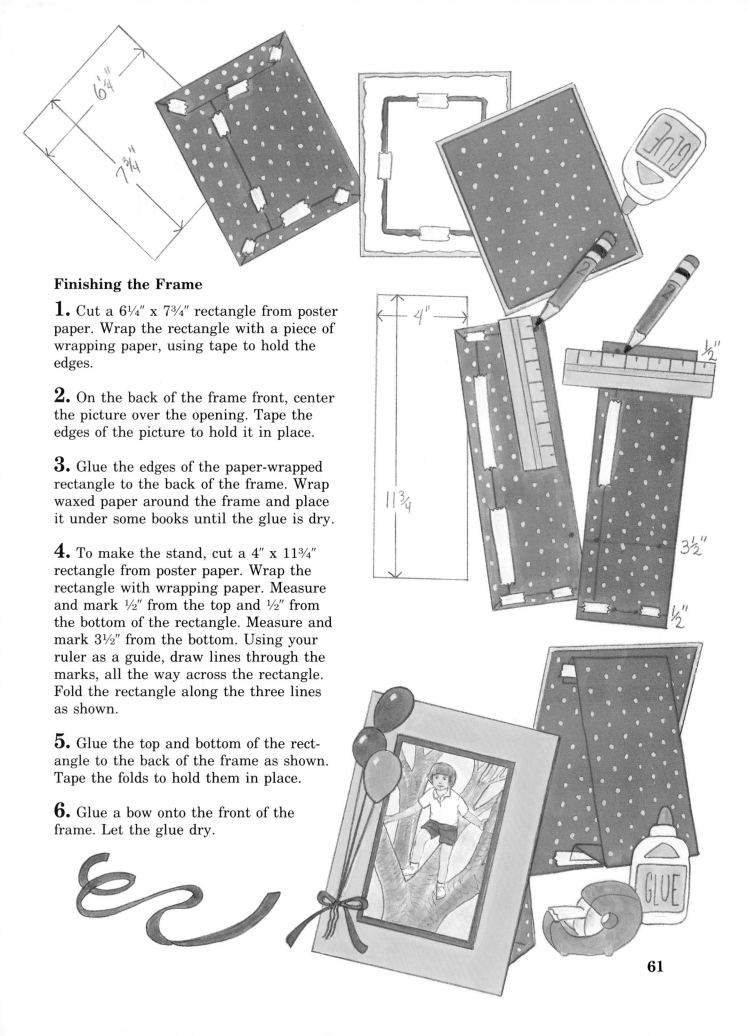

Finishing the Frame

1. Cut a 6¼″ x 7¾″ rectangle from poster paper. Wrap the rectangle with a piece of wrapping paper, using tape to hold the edges.

2. On the back of the frame front, center the picture over the opening. Tape the edges of the picture to hold it in place.

3. Glue the edges of the paper-wrapped rectangle to the back of the frame. Wrap waxed paper around the frame and place it under some books until the glue is dry.

4. To make the stand, cut a 4″ x 11¾″ rectangle from poster paper. Wrap the rectangle with wrapping paper. Measure and mark ½″ from the top and ½″ from the bottom of the rectangle. Measure and mark 3½″ from the bottom. Using your ruler as a guide, draw lines through the marks, all the way across the rectangle. Fold the rectangle along the three lines as shown.

5. Glue the top and bottom of the rectangle to the back of the frame as shown. Tape the folds to hold them in place.

6. Glue a bow onto the front of the frame. Let the glue dry.

61

Toys Ahoy

Here are some toys that float. Make a tubful! They're easy to cut out and fun to paint.

You will need:
pencil
tracing paper
scissors
plastic foam plates
acrylic paint
paintbrush
dinner knife

1. Trace all of the patterns and cut them out.

2. Draw around the patterns on the plates. (You'll need one base for each toy that you make.) Draw the features. Cut out the plastic foam pieces.

3. Paint the pieces. Let the paint dry.

4. Use the knife to cut a slit in each base. Slip the toys into the bases.

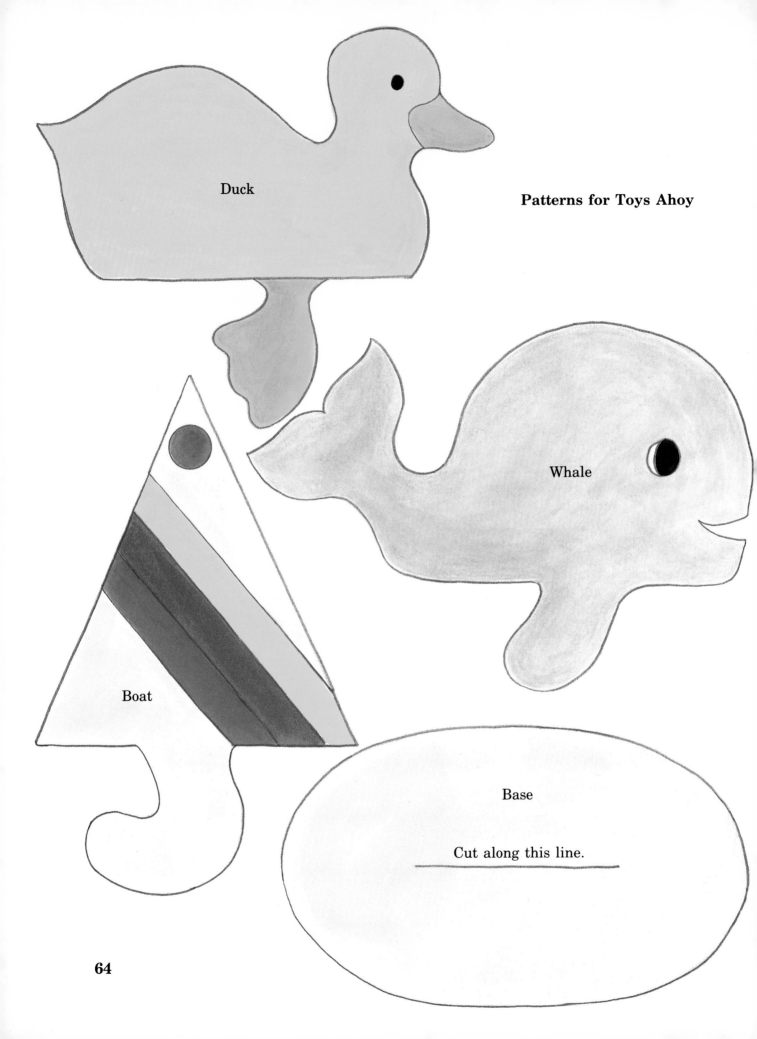

Duck

Patterns for Toys Ahoy

Whale

Boat

Base

Cut along this line.

64

Message Minders

Make these handy holders in minutes. Draw and paint your own designs or use the ones shown here.

For safety's sake: Be sure to follow the directions on the back of the can of spray enamel. Ask a grown-up to read these with you and to help if you need it.

You will need:
clothespins
newspaper
clear plastic spray enamel
enamel paint and brush, paint pens, or
    permanent fine-tip markers
tiny stickers
magnetic tape (self-adhesive)

1. Place the clothespins on several sheets of newspaper. Lightly spray the clothespins with the clear plastic enamel. Let dry.

2. Paint designs on the clothespins, or decorate them with stickers. Let the paint dry.

3. Cut a piece of magnetic tape to stick on the back of each clothespin.

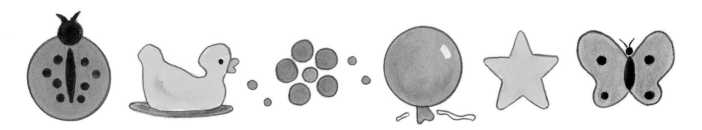

Clay Candlesticks

Mold a family of candlesticks for a family you know. See if they can guess who's who!

You will need:
newspaper
package of self-hardening clay
bowl of water
small sponge
modeling tools (toothpicks, pencil, spoon)
garlic press
candle

1. Cover your work area with plenty of newspaper and roll up your sleeves.

2. Pull off a small piece of clay and roll it into a coil that is 10″ to 11″ long. Pinch the ends of the coil together to make a circle.

3. Roll another coil that is a little shorter than the first one and pinch the ends together. Place this coil on top of the first one. Dampen your fingers or the sponge with water and smooth the edges of the coils together.

4. Keep rolling and stacking coils. Remember to roll each new coil a little shorter than the last one and to smooth the edges together.

5. When you have enough coils for the body, roll a small ball of clay for the head. Put the head on the body and smooth the line to make a neck. Roll a coil and cut it in half for the arms. Stick the arms on the body and smooth the tops of them to make shoulders.

6. Add special touches, like clay buttons or a clay belt. If you like, make something fun for your figure to hold—maybe a ball, a doll, or even a flower.

7. Using a toothpick or pencil, poke holes for the eyes and mouth. Press tiny circles of clay onto the head for cheeks. Make hair by braiding small coils or squeezing some clay through the garlic press.

8. Roll a coil that will fit around the candle. Put the coil on top of the head and press gently.

9. Put the candle holder in a sunny spot and let it dry for several days.

PARENTS' WORKSHOP
Great Gifts for Children

Satchel Set

With satchel, lunch sack, and pencil case in hand, a youngster just starting school will be all set—and happy to go!

Note: Use ½″ seam allowance throughout unless instructed otherwise. When pressing vinyl-coated fabric, use a pressing cloth.

Satchel

You will need:
⅔ yard vinyl-coated khaki fabric
⅔ yard green fabric (for lining and windows)
⅔ yard fusible interfacing
7″ x 9″ piece of red fabric
thread to match khaki and red fabrics
small pieces of blue, yellow, and black fabric
¼ yard fusible web
1⅓ yards (1″-wide) red grosgrain ribbon
3 pairs of Velcro fasteners (medium duty)

1. From khaki fabric, cut one 15″ x 33″ rectangle for satchel front, bottom, back, and flap (Figure A) and two 3½″ x 10½″ strips for satchel sides. From lining and from fusible interfacing, cut one 15″ x 33″ rectangle.

2. On the wrong side of the large khaki rectangle, measure 10″ and 13″ from one end and draw lines across width of fabric as shown. (Figure A.) Fold the rectangle along the lines, wrong sides together, and press. On right side, sew a ⅛″ seam along each fold to form the satchel bottom.

3. With right sides together and raw edges aligned, center and pin one end of each side strip to the satchel bottom between the ⅛″ seams; sew. Pin side of each strip to satchel front and sew. Trim seams. Fold down top edge of satchel front and sides ½″ and press. (Figure B.)

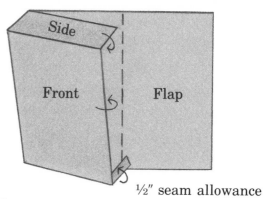

½″ seam allowance

Figure B

4. Fuse interfacing to wrong side of lining, following manufacturer's instructions. With right sides together and raw edges aligned, pin one end of the lining to side and bottom edges of the satchel flap. Sew as shown. (Figure A.) Trim seams. Turn under side edges of the remaining lining ½″ and press; sew ¼″ from each folded edge.

Sew one end of lining between Xs.

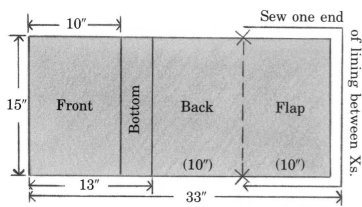

Figure A

5. Trace and cut out the patterns for the large car. For each pattern piece, simultaneously cut one from color fabric indicated and one from fusible web. With fabric piece on top of fusible web piece, center the car body on right side of satchel flap, 2¼″ from bottom edge, and pin. Position and pin remaining pieces. Fuse the pieces, following instructions of fusible web manufacturer.

6. Set sewing machine for appliqué. (Consult your sewing machine handbook for best results.) Using red thread, appliqué the pieces.

7. With right sides together and raw edges aligned, pin remaining sides of side strips to satchel back and sew. Trim seams and turn satchel right side out.

8. Place loose end of lining inside satchel, folding under raw edge of lining to meet top edge of satchel front. Pin front edges of satchel and lining together and sew, stitching close to top edge. Sew again, stitching ¼″ from first seam.

9. Sew the Velcro fasteners 1″ above bottom of satchel front and to underside of satchel flap, spacing fasteners evenly.

Cut ribbon in half. Align ribbon halves and pin together; sew long edges, stitching close to the edges. On right side of satchel sides, center and pin ribbon ends ½″ from top edges; attach ribbon ends to satchel sides with two rows of zigzag stitching.

Pattern for Small Car

Lunch Bag

You will need:
½ yard vinyl-coated khaki fabric
small pieces of green, blue, red, yellow, and black fabric
thread to match khaki and green fabric
fusible web
pinking shears
2 pairs of Velcro fasteners (medium duty)

1. From khaki fabric, cut one 9½″ x 28″ rectangle and two 4½″ x 12½″ strips.

2. On wrong side of the large khaki rectangle, measure 12″ and 16″ from one end and draw lines across the width of the fabric. Fold the rectangle along the lines, wrong sides together, and press. On right side, sew a ⅛″ seam along each fold to form bag bottom.

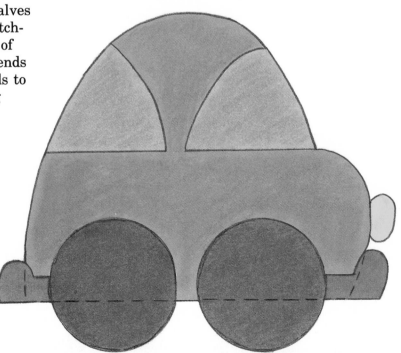

3. Trace and cut out the patterns for the small car. For each pattern piece, simultaneously cut one from color fabric indicated and one from fusible web.

Turn large khaki rectangle right side up with one 9½″ end at top. With fabric piece on top of fusible web piece, center car on khaki rectangle with car top 6″ from top edge; pin. Position and pin remaining pieces. Fuse the pieces, following instructions of fusible web manufacturer.

4. Set sewing machine for appliqué. (Consult your sewing machine handbook for best results.) Using green thread, appliqué the pieces.

5. With right sides together, center and pin one 4½″ end of one khaki strip to the bottom of the bag; repeat for remaining khaki strip. Pin the sides of the strips to the front and back of the bag. Sew the strips to the bag. Trim seams and turn bag right side out.

6. Evenly trim the top edges of the bag with pinking shears. On back of bag, sew Velcro fasteners near top edge, 1″ from each side seam. On front of bag, sew remaining fasteners 2¼″ from top edge, 1″ from side seams. With edges together, fold down top of bag 1″ and press. Fold down top again so that fasteners meet; press. (Figure C.)

Pencil Case

You will need:
¼ yard vinyl-coated khaki
¼ yard red fabric
small pieces of blue, green, yellow, and black fabric
fusible web
thread to match blue fabric
9″ red zipper
5″ (⅛″-wide) ribbon

1. From khaki fabric and red fabric, cut two 6″ x 10″ rectangles. Pin the khaki rectangles to the red rectangles, wrong sides together.

2. Trace and cut out the patterns for the small car. Simultaneously cut pieces from fabric (see photograph for colors) and fusible web. With fabric piece on top of fusible web piece, center car body on front (khaki side) of one rectangle and pin; position and pin remaining pieces. Fuse the pieces, following instructions of fusible web manufacturer.

3. With right sides together and raw edges aligned, pin one side of zipper tape to top of case front; sew, stitching close to the zipper. Pin remaining side of zipper tape to case back and sew. Press seams flat against red lining; topstitch ¼″ from seam.

Open the zipper halfway. With right sides together and raw edges aligned, pin case front to case back; sew all around. Trim seams; turn case and press. Tie ribbon onto zipper pull.

Figure C

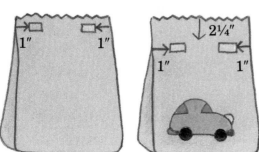

Back   Front

Fold down 1″.

Fold again to close.

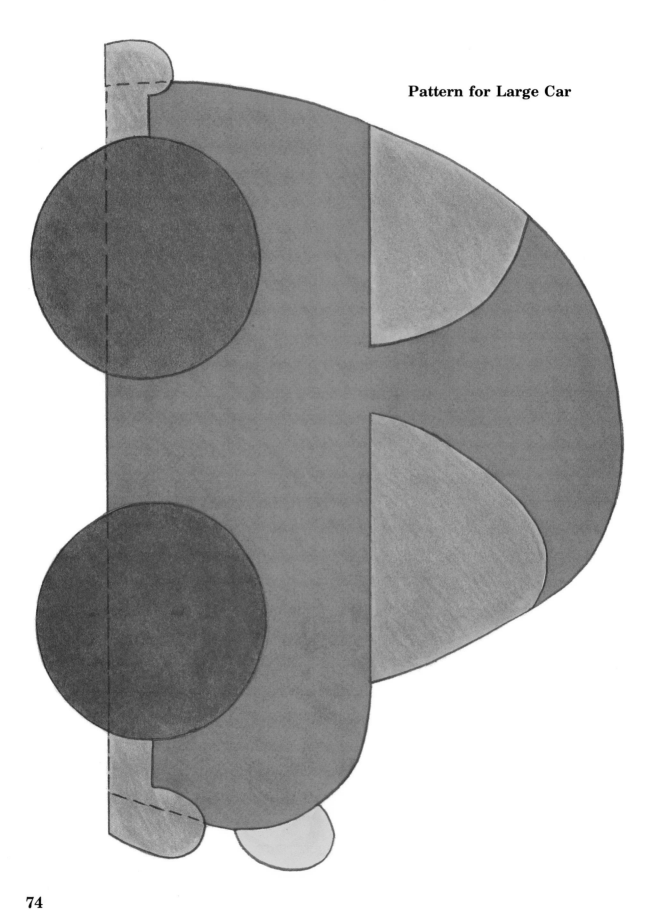

Pattern for Large Car

Dinosaur Peg Rack

A twinkling eye and an ear-to-ear grin make this fellow irresistible to kids. Once he's up, you'll find fewer "lost" mittens, mufflers, and such.

You will need:
tracing paper
carbon paper
1 (2-foot) 1 x 12
band saw (or jigsaw)
electric drill with ½″ bit
sandpaper
clear acrylic spray enamel
acrylic paint
paintbrushes
2 sawtooth picture hangers
3 (½″-diameter and 3″-long) wooden
   dowels
white glue

1. Trace the outline of the dinosaur. Reverse the tracing and transfer the outline to the back (rough side) of the 1 x 12, using carbon paper and a pencil. Cut out the dinosaur with the band saw.

2. On the front (smooth side) of the dinosaur, use the drill to make ½″ holes for the dowels, as marked on the pattern. Sand the front and back of the dinosaur and the cut edges. Spray with clear acrylic enamel; let dry and sand lightly.

3. Apply one coat of paint to the back of the dinosaur and let dry. Attach the picture hangers as marked.

Match Xs and continue pattern across page.

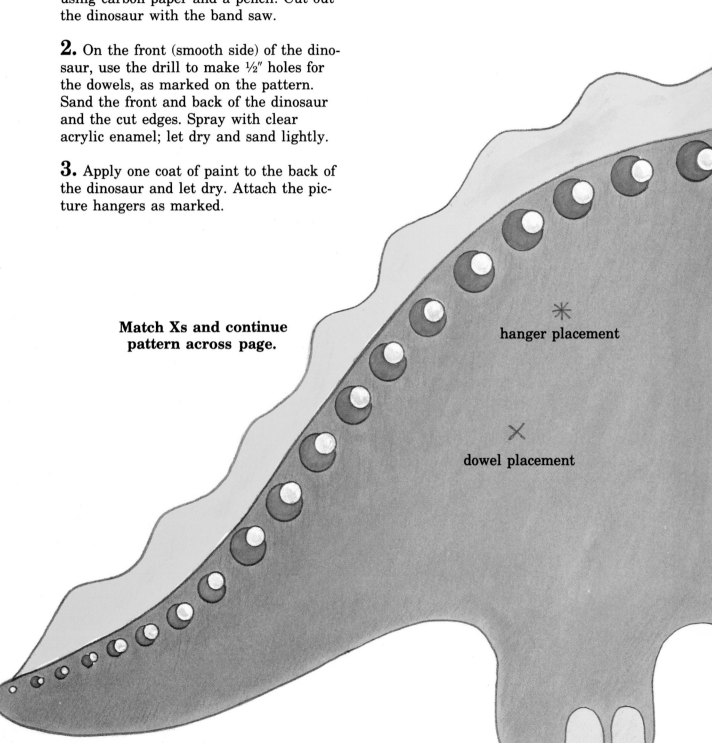

hanger placement

dowel placement

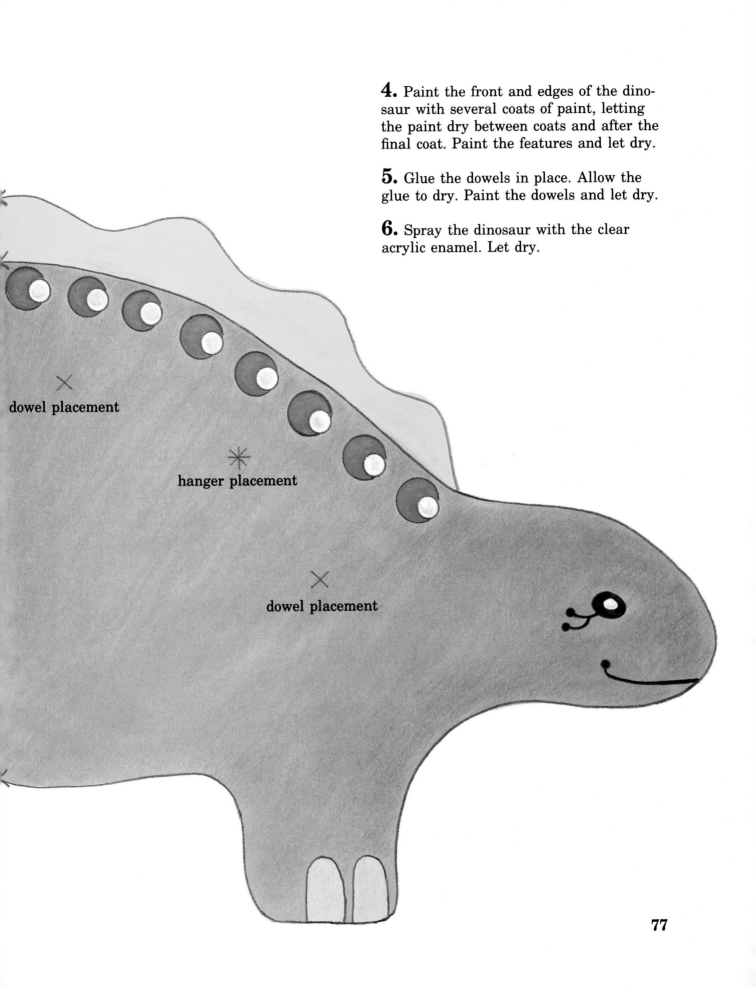

4. Paint the front and edges of the dinosaur with several coats of paint, letting the paint dry between coats and after the final coat. Paint the features and let dry.

5. Glue the dowels in place. Allow the glue to dry. Paint the dowels and let dry.

6. Spray the dinosaur with the clear acrylic enamel. Let dry.

dowel placement

hanger placement

dowel placement

Jiffy Gym Bag

Although designed with sports in mind, this roomy bag will catch and carry all—from balls and books to games, pj's, and toys.

You will need:
tracing paper
¼ yard (45″-wide) striped fabric
⅛ yard (45″-wide) pale pink fabric
⅛ yard (45″-wide) white fabric
⅛ yard (45″-wide) red fabric
1 yard fusible web
⅔ yard (45″-wide) blue fabric
thread to match fabrics
2 yards thick white cording

1. Trace and cut out the patterns for the shoe, sole, and laces. From fabric and fusible web, cut two for each pattern piece.

Trace and cut out the patterns for the leg and shorts. Cut pieces as marked.

2. To cuff legs of shorts, lay the shorts wrong side up. Turn up bottom edge of one leg ¼"; press and sew. Turn up leg 1½" from fold and press. Fold up cuff 1" to right side of shorts and press. Repeat for remaining leg.

3. Open blue fabric, right side up, and lay flat with 45" side at top. With fabric pieces on top of fusible web pieces, center legs on blue fabric as shown. Place shorts on top of legs and adjust legs if necessary. Remove shorts and pin the legs. Position and pin shoes, soles, and laces, referring to photograph for placement. Following instructions of fusible web manufacturer, fuse pieces to bag.

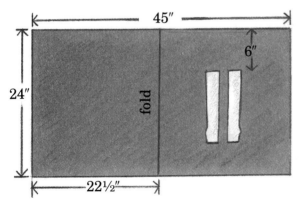

4. Set sewing machine for appliqué. (Consult your sewing machine handbook for best results.) Using matching thread, appliqué the pieces.

5. With top edges aligned, position the shorts on the blue fabric. Appliqué the legs of the shorts, stitching along the outer and inner sides. (Do not stitch bottom or top edges of the shorts.)

6. To make the casing, lay the blue fabric wrong side up. Turn down top edge ½" and press; turn down edge 1½" and sew, stitching close to the edge.

7. Fold blue fabric on fold line (see figure) with right sides together. Sew bottom and side, using ½" seam allowance and leaving ends of casing free. Turn bag right side out and press. Pull the cording through the casing; knot the ends.

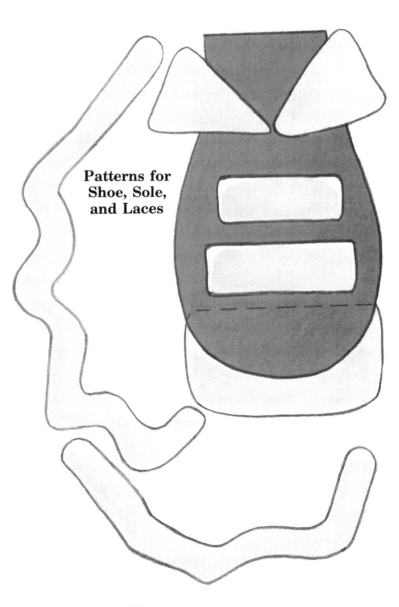

Patterns for Shoe, Sole, and Laces

**Match Xs and continue
pattern across page.**

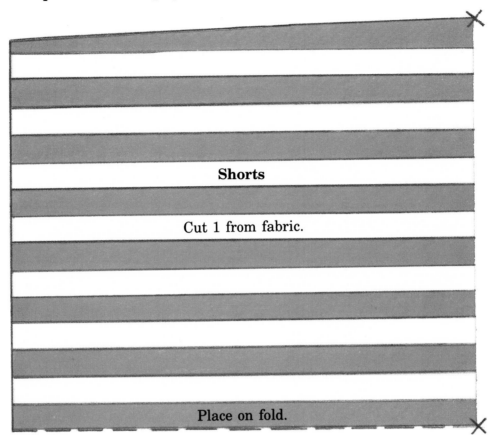

Shorts

Cut 1 from fabric.

Place on fold.

Leg

Cut 1 from fabric; reverse, cut 1.
Cut 2 from fusible web.

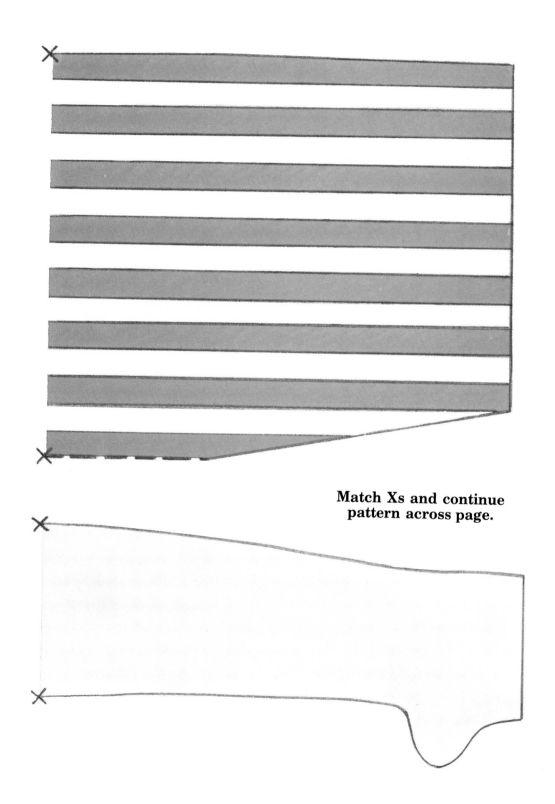

**Match Xs and continue
pattern across page.**

Book Nook

This kitty's favorite pastime? Cat-napping, of course, while minding books that are not in use. Adjustable, the wooden rack will look mighty sweet on a child's desk or bedside table.

You will need:
tracing paper
1 (3-foot) 1 x 12
band saw (or jigsaw)
sandpaper
electric drill with ⅜″ and ½″ bits
wood glue
3 (⅜″-diameter and 11″-long) wooden
  dowels
clear acrylic spray enamel
paintbrushes
gloss enamel paint (white, pink, gray,
  blue, yellow, and green)

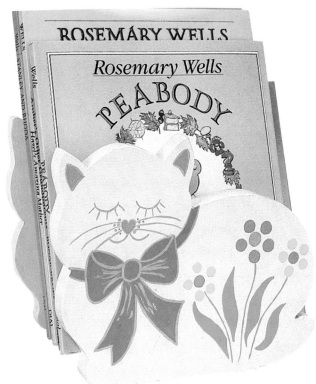

1. Trace the pattern, including features and hole placement marks (Xs), onto tracing paper. Cut out the pattern. Mark the front of the pattern A and the back B.

2. On the rough side of the 1 x 12, draw around side A of the pattern for the back cat. For the front cat, draw around side B. Cut out the cats with the saw.

3. Sand the fronts, backs, and edges of the cats. Using carbon paper and pencil, transfer hole placement marks to the rough side of each cat.

4. Using the drill and ⅜″ bit, drill holes ½″ deep in the rough side of the front cat. Using the ½″ bit, drill holes completely through the back cat.

5. Put several drops of glue in each hole in the front cat and insert a dowel. Let the glue dry.

6. Spray entire book rack with clear acrylic; let dry and sand lightly. Paint the book rack with several coats of white paint, allowing the paint to dry between coats and after the final coat.

7. Transfer features to the front cat, using carbon paper and pencil. Paint the features as indicated on the pattern. Let dry. Assemble the book rack.

Shoe-Choo Train

Handy for holding shoes, as well as a young man's treasures, this appliquéd bag features sixteen pockets and a heart-chugging choo-choo train.

You will need:

tape measure
1 yard (45″-wide) bleached muslin
1½ yards red plaid fabric
tracing paper
⅛ yard blue fabric
small piece of pink fabric
⅛ yard yellow fabric
⅛ yard red fabric
⅓ yard fusible web
thread to match fabrics
needles (sewing, embroidery, and quilting)
embroidery floss (navy blue, yellow, pink,
    and yellow-orange)
1 yard silver elastic thread
yellow candlewicking thread (or cotton
    yarn)
9″ narrow pink ribbon
small buttons (6 white hearts, 1 white
    bow, 1 red bow, and 3 yellow stars)
water-soluble marking pen
22″ x 40″ piece of fleece
white quilting thread
18″ (⅜″-diameter) wooden dowel

Cutting the Pieces

1. From bleached muslin, cut one 13¼″ x 20″ rectangle (for appliqué), one 22″ x 40″ rectangle (for bag backing), and one 1¾″ x 19½″ strip (for dowel casing).

2. From red plaid fabric, cut one 20½″ x 26½″ rectangle (for bag), four 6¾″ x 28½″ strips (for pockets), two 1½″ x 4″ strips (for hangers), and 3⅓ yards of 1½″-wide bias strips (for binding).

Making the Appliqué

1. Trace and cut out the pattern pieces. For each pattern piece, simultaneously cut one from fabric and one from fusible web.

2. With fabric piece on top of fusible web piece, position the engine on the 13¼″ x 20″ muslin rectangle as indicated on the pattern and pin. Position and pin remaining pieces, referring to the photograph and patterns for placement. (Broken lines indicate overlapping and underlapping of appliqué pieces.) Following instructions of fusible web manufacturer, fuse the pieces.

3. Set sewing machine for appliqué. (Consult your sewing machine handbook for best results.) Appliqué the pieces, using matching thread and satin stitch. Satin-stitch lion, bear, and engineer's hat, as marked on patterns.

4. Using two strands of embroidery floss and referring to patterns for placement, embroider the following details: on the engineer's face, navy blue backstitch for nose and French knots for eyes; on the lion, yellow-orange satin stitch for tip of nose and chain stitch for outline of nose and mouth; on the bear's face, pink French knots for eyes; around the wheels, navy blue buttonhole stitch. Embroider the balloons as indicated on the patterns, using two strands of yellow floss.

5. Cut the elastic thread into three pieces and knot one end of each. Using the embroidery needle, run the threads under the engineer's hand. (See pattern.) Knot remaining ends of threads and tack to balloons. Gently pull the threads to curve them.

6. To form the lion's mane and tail, make ¼″ loops with the candlewicking thread and tack the loops in place with yellow sewing thread. (See pattern.)

7. Tie pink ribbon into bow and tack to bear under chin. Sew bow buttons onto engineer and lion, heart buttons onto wheels, and star buttons onto last train car, as indicated by Xs on pattern.

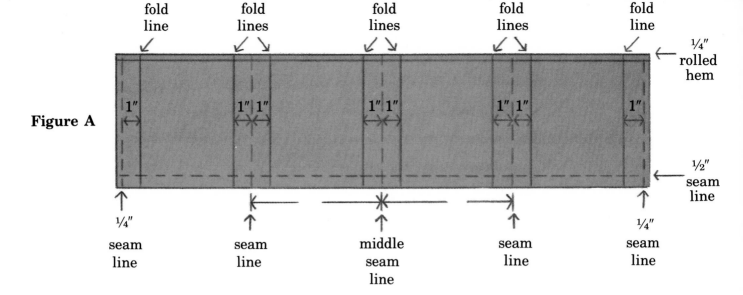

Figure A

fold line   fold lines   fold lines   fold lines   fold line

1″   1″ 1″   1″ 1″   1″ 1″   1″

¼″ rolled hem

½″ seam line

¼″ seam line   seam line   middle seam line   seam line   ¼″ seam line

Sewing the Pockets

1. At the top (one long edge) of each pocket strip, sew a ¼″ rolled hem.

2. Using the water-soluble pen, mark a ¼″ seam line along the ends of the strips and a ½″ seam line along the bottom of the strips. Fold each strip in half with the ends together; draw a seam line down the middle, from the top of the strip to the bottom. On either side of the middle seam line, measure 7″ and draw a seam line from top to bottom. For fold lines, measure 1″ on either side of the three center seam lines and 1″ from the ¼″ seam lines at ends. Draw lines from top to bottom. (Figure A.)

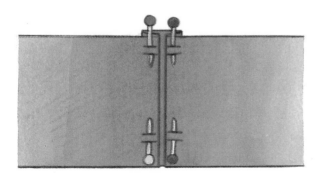

Figure B

3. On each pocket strip, fold and press all fold lines (wrong sides together), allowing folds to fall open after pressing. Lay strips right side up. To form pleats on each strip, bring the pressed fold lines to the marked seam lines and pin. (Figure B.) Press.

4. With right sides together and raw edges aligned, pin one short end of the large plaid rectangle to the bottom of the appliquéd muslin rectangle; sew, using ¼″ seam allowance. Press the seam toward the plaid rectangle.

On the front of the plaid rectangle, measure 7″, 13″, 19″, and 25″ from the seam and draw seam lines from side to side with the water-soluble pen. Fold the rectangle in half lengthwise and mark the center of each seam line; on either side of the center marks, measure and mark 5″. (Figure C.)

5. With wrong side up and rolled hem toward bottom, place one pocket strip on right side of plaid rectangle, aligning ½″ seam line on bottom of strip with 7″ line on rectangle and aligning vertical seam lines on strips with vertical marks on rectangle. (Figures A and C.) Carefully pin the strip to the bag along the 7″ line and sew. Remove pins and press pockets up. Repeat for remaining strips, sewing strips to bag along 13″, 19″, and 25″ lines.

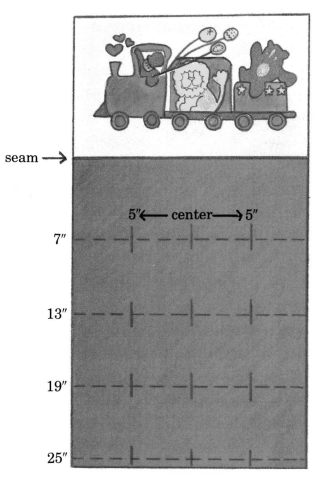

seam →

5″ ← center → 5″

7″

13″

19″

25″

Figure C

6. To complete pockets, sew strips to bag along vertical seam lines, stitching from top to bottom of each strip.

Finishing the Shoe Bag

1. Place the fleece rectangle on top of the 22″ x 40″ muslin rectangle and center the shoe bag, right side up, on top. Pin the three layers together along the vertical seam lines; baste, then machine-stitch, from top to bottom of bag.

2. Hand-quilt (or machine-stitch with white thread) around the train, bear, balloon, and hearts.

3. To make the hangers, fold one 1½″ x 4″ rectangle with right sides and long edges together. Sew a ¼″ seam along the long raw edges. Turn the hanger right side out and press. Topstitch both long edges, stitching close to the edges. Repeat for remaining 1½″ x 4″ rectangle. Loop hangers and baste ends to top front of shoe bag, with raw edges aligned.

4. Make a continuous bias strip. Beginning at the lower right-hand corner, pin the bias strip to the front edge of the shoe bag, with right sides together and raw edges aligned. Machine-stitch, using ¼″ seam allowance.

Trim fleece and muslin backing to match raw edges of shoe bag. Fold bias around raw edges to back of shoe bag. Tuck under raw edge of bias to cover stitching line; blind-stitch. Tack hangers to top of binding.

5. On the front of the appliquéd muslin rectangle, hand-quilt (or machine-stitch with white thread) along all four sides, stitching ¼″ from the edge.

6. To make the dowel casing, sew a ⅜″ rolled hem at the ends (short edges) of the 1¾″ x 19½″ muslin rectangle. Turn under the long edges ¼″, wrong sides together, and press. Position top of casing just under the bias binding at top of bag. Blind-stitch casing to back of shoe bag. Insert the dowel.

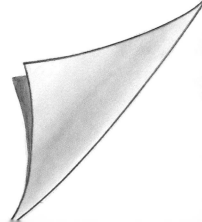

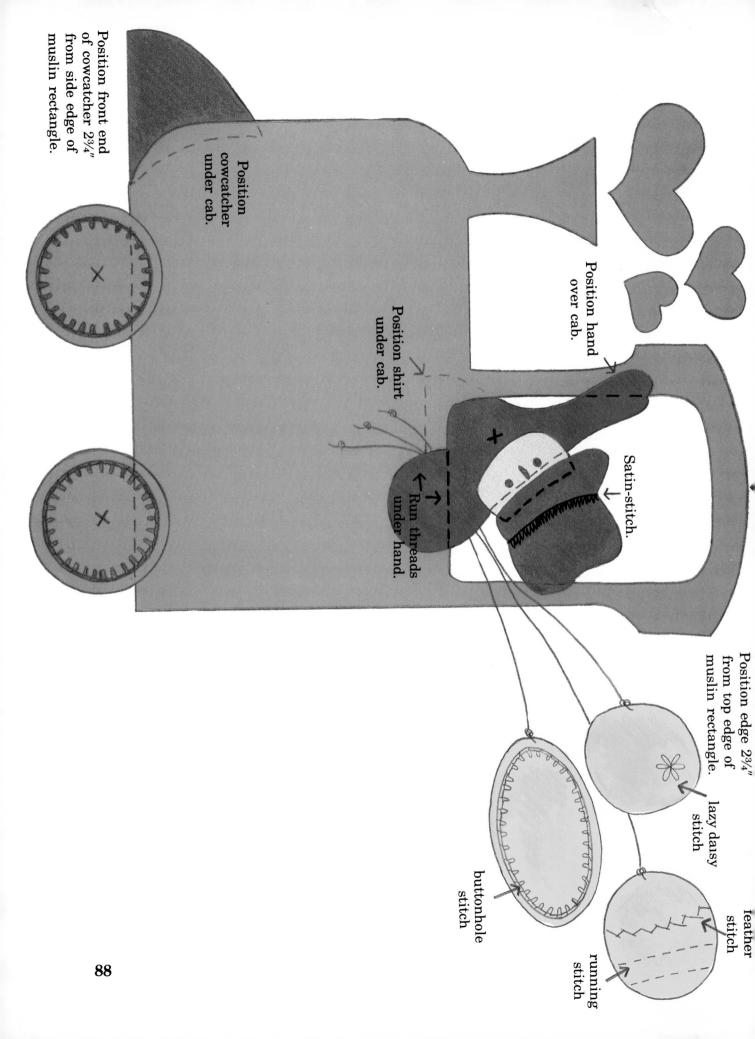

Position front end
of cowcatcher 2¾″
from side edge of
muslin rectangle.

Position
cowcatcher
under cab.

Position shirt
under cab.

Position hand
over cab.

Satin-stitch.

←Run threads
under hand.

Position edge 2¾″
from top edge of
muslin rectangle.

lazy daisy
stitch

feather
stitch

buttonhole
stitch

running
stitch

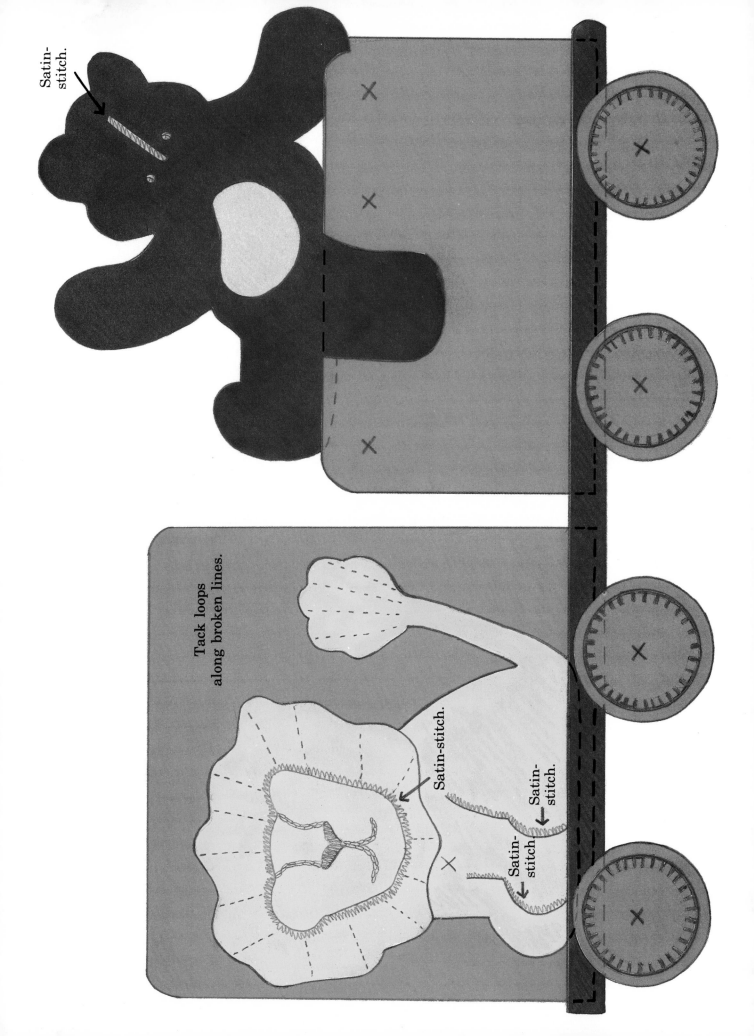

Satin-stitch.

Tack loops along broken lines.

Satin-stitch.

Satin-stitch.

Satin-stitch.

Ruffled Sweatshirts

Ruffles add a distinctively feminine and festive touch to these holiday shirts. No doubt you know a little girl who'd be tickled to have one. (Her mother would probably love one, too!)

Candy Cane Sweatshirt

You will need:
white sweatshirt
⅜ yard white sweatshirt fabric
  (fleece-lined)
white thread
tracing paper
1¾ yards (1″-wide) green polka-dot ribbon
water-soluble marking pen
red and green acrylic (or fabric) paint
paintbrush
transparent nylon thread

1. Wash and dry the sweatshirt.

2. Fold the sweatshirt neck ribbing in half, toward inside of the shirt, and pin. Machine-stitch around the ribbing.

3. From the sweatshirt fabric, cut approximately 50 strips, cutting each strip 1½″ wide and 7″ long. (The number and size of strips needed will vary according to the size of the sweatshirt. The sweatshirts shown are small and medium adult-size shirts. For a smaller shirt, cut smaller and fewer strips.)

4. Pin a row of strips around the neck ribbing, spacing the strips about ½″ apart and placing the centers of the strips on the center of the ribbing. Machine-stitch around the ribbing, sewing through the centers of the strips. (Figure A.)

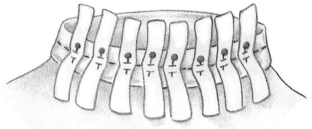

Figure A

Turn first row of strips up and out of the way. Pin second row of strips as indicated by first row of Xs, placing centers of second-row strips ½″ below ribbing. (Figure B.) Machine-stitch through centers of second-row strips, sewing one continuous line around shirt.

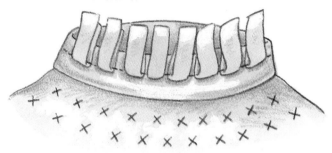

Figure B

If desired, add a third row of strips to the front of the shirt only. Pin third-row strips as indicated by second row of Xs, placing centers of third-row strips ½″ below centers of second-row strips. (Figure B.) Machine-stitch through centers of third-row strips, sewing one continuous line across front of shirt.

5. Tie the strips into knots.

6. Trace and cut out the candy cane pattern. Using the water-soluble pen, draw around the candy cane on the front of the shirt, referring to photograph for placement. Draw stripes on the candy canes.

7. Outline the candy canes with the red paint. Paint the stripes red and green. Allow the paint to dry overnight.

8. Cut the ribbon into 14″ lengths. To make bows, fold the ends of each ribbon toward the center and cross the ends. (Figure C.) Tightly wrap a piece of transparent thread around the center of the bow and tie the ends of the thread. Sew bows to centers of candy canes, using the transparent thread.

Figure C

Christmas Tree Sweatshirt

You will need:
red sweatshirt
⅜ yard red sweatshirt fabric (fleece-lined)
10″ x 11″ piece of washable green felt
scraps of washable felt in assorted colors
thread to match sweatshirt and felts
tracing paper
sequins in assorted shapes, sizes, and
  colors
transparent nylon thread
scraps of ribbon

1. Wash, dry, and press all the felt pieces.

2. Follow steps 1 through 5 in directions for candy cane sweatshirt.

3. Trace and cut out the tree and star patterns. Cut the tree from green felt and the star from yellow felt. From remaining felt scraps, cut pieces for the packages.

4. Sew sequins to the tree, using the transparent thread.

5. Center the tree on the front of the sweatshirt and pin. Using green thread, machine-stitch edges of tree. Position and pin the packages and star; machine-stitch edges, using matching thread.

6. Tie bows with the ribbon scraps and tack to the packages.

Note: To launder finished sweatshirt, turn the sweatshirt inside out; machine-wash in cold water on gentle cycle. Hang to dry.

Place on fold.

93

Mary's Little Lamb Collar

Pretty as a picture, this dainty collar is surprisingly simple to stitch. Worked on white Linda 27 over two threads, the finished design measures 9⅛" x 5½". The fabric was cut 12" x 16". To determine the cross-stitch fabric to be used for other design sizes, refer to the chart on the following page.

You will need:
purchased collar pattern (with straight
   edge on front)
tape measure
cross-stitch fabric
embroidery floss (in colors indicated on
   color key)
embroidery needle

1. From the cross-stitch fabric, cut a rectangle that is 3" bigger all around than the collar pattern.

2. Measure 3" in from the left side of the fabric rectangle and 3" up from the bottom. Begin stitching, following the graph and color key.

3. When stitching is complete, center the collar pattern over the design and pin; cut the collar. Follow pattern instructions to complete the collar.

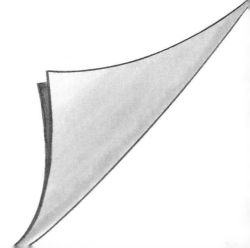

DMC **Color Key**

Cross-stitch (two strands)

	·	╱	White
726	△	◢	Topaz-lt.
725	▲	◢	Topaz
963	—		Dusty Rose-vy. lt.
3687	■		Mauve
309	□		Rose-deep
827	✕		Blue-vy. lt.
518	○		Wedgewood-lt.
792	●	◢	Cornflower Blue-dk.
955	·		Nile Green-lt.
992	○		Aquamarine
842		╱	Beige Brown-vy. lt.
841	✕		Beige Brown-lt.

Backstitch (one strand)

3687	Mauve (flower stems in dress, bow on sheep)
992	Aquamarine (remaining flower stems)
414	Steel Gray-dk. (all else)

French Knots (one strand)

414	●	Steel Gray-dk.

Fabric	Design Size
Aida 11	11⅛″ x 6⅞″
Aida 14	8¾″ x 5⅜″
Aida 18	6⅞″ x 4⅛″
Hardanger 22	5⅝″ x 3⅜″

Giraffe Overalls

Liven up a pair of plain overalls with a long-on-good-looks giraffe. When buying the overalls, choose a pair with a pocket (for the leaf appliqués) and an inner leg seam that can be easily opened.

You will need:
pair of overalls
tracing paper
⅓ yard yellow polka-dot fabric
scrap of green polka-dot fabric
½ yard fusible web
½ yard tear-away backing for appliqué
⅓ yard orange drapery fringe
thread (yellow, orange, blue, white, and green)
water-soluble marking pen

Front

Back

1. Trace and cut out the appliqué patterns. Cut giraffe from yellow polka-dot and fusible web. Cut leaves from green polka-dot and fusible web. From tear-away backing, cut one 11″ x 16″ rectangle to back the giraffe and one small piece to back the leaves.

2. Cut a 7″ piece of drapery fringe. Beginning at point indicated on pattern, hand-baste the fringe along the giraffe's head and neck.

3. Open inside seam of right pant leg. With fabric giraffe on top of fusible web giraffe, position pieces on pant leg, referring to photographs for placement. Fuse the giraffe, following instructions of fusible web manufacturer.

4. On wrong side of pant leg, position tear-away backing directly behind giraffe. Set machine for appliqué. (Consult sewing machine handbook for best results.) Using

satin stitch and yellow thread, machine-appliqué the giraffe.

Use the marking pen to draw the giraffe's nose, eye, tip of tail, and hooves. Satin-stitch nose, tail, and hooves, using orange thread; satin-stitch eye, using blue thread and white thread. Carefully tear away the backing.

5. Cut a ½″ piece of fringe. Machine-stitch the fringe between the giraffe's horns, with ends of fringe pointed toward giraffe's nose.

6. With fabric leaves on top of fusible web leaves, position pieces on pocket, referring to photograph for placement. Place the small piece of tear-away backing inside the pocket, behind the leaves. Using satin stitch and green thread, machine-appliqué the leaves. Carefully tear away the backing.

7. Sew leg seam closed.

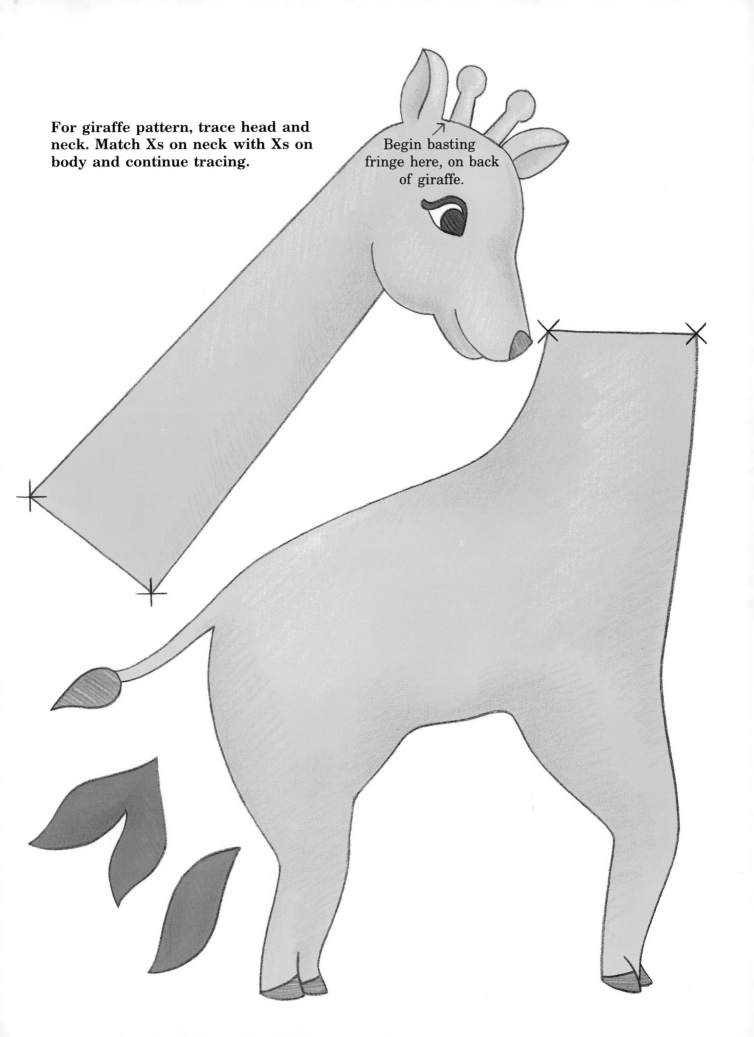

For giraffe pattern, trace head and neck. Match Xs on neck with Xs on body and continue tracing.

Begin basting fringe here, on back of giraffe.

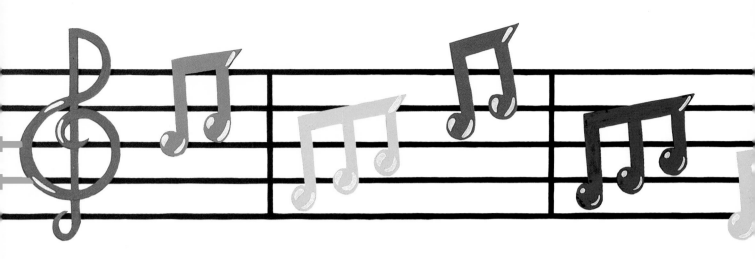

100

Noteworthy Suspenders

Tack simple-to-appliqué shapes to suspenders for gifts that are fun—and functional, too!

You will need (for each pair):
tracing paper
dressmakers' carbon
6″ x 12″ piece of fusible web, plus small scraps
6″ x 12″ piece of muslin
6″ x 12″ piece of fleece
For the dogs: ¼ yard brown print fabric, scraps of pink and black fabric, black and brown thread, 12 black beads, ribbon for bows (optional), blue suspenders
For the stars: ¼ yard pale yellow fabric, aqua and pale yellow thread, 20 silver beads, 4 small black buttons, aqua embroidery floss, aqua suspenders
For the trees: ¼ yard green fabric, scraps of red and brown fabric, green and white thread, 24 red beads, 6 white heart buttons, 2 yellow star buttons, 2 red star buttons, 6 silver star sequins, red suspenders

1. Trace and cut out the pattern for the dog, star, or tree.

2. From ¼ yard fabric, cut two 6″ x 12″ rectangles. For design fronts, transfer the pattern two times to the right side of one fabric rectangle, using dressmakers' carbon and pencil.

3. From fabric and fusible web scraps, cut the small shapes (trunk and pot for each tree; nose, eyes, and ears for each dog). Position the shapes on the patterns drawn on the fabric rectangle. Fuse the pieces, according to instructions of fusible web manufacturer.

4. Layer, then fuse, the piece of muslin, the 6″ x 12″ piece of fusible web, and the decorated fabric rectangle (right side up).

5. Layer the plain fabric rectangle (wrong side up), the piece of fleece, and the decorated fabric rectangle (muslin side down); pin, then hand-baste, the layers together.

6. Set sewing machine for appliqué. (Consult sewing machine handbook for best results.) Using satin stitch, machine-appliqué the small shapes (on tree and dog) and outline the main shape as shown on pattern. Cut out the main shapes. Satin-stitch the shapes again, as above, to fill in the stitches and cover raw edges.

7. Using thread to match fabric, sew buttons, beads, and sequins to main shapes as indicated on pattern. On stars, satin-stitch hearts and mouth, using four strands of embroidery floss; backstitch the smile and eyebrows.

8. Adjust suspenders to fit child and pin finished shapes in place. Tack the shapes to the suspenders.

Reindeer Apron

Cute as a button, this pinafore-style apron will keep clothes clean while a little one cooks or entertains guests. For a soft and pudgy look, lightly stuff the reindeer's face and nose with polyester stuffing. Sew one floppy ear up and one down for whimsy.

104

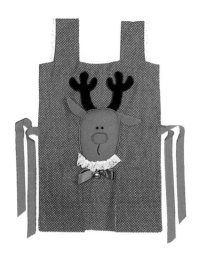

You will need:

1 yard (45″-wide) red polka-dot fabric
1 yard (45″-wide) red striped fabric
thread (red, gray, and black)
⅔ yard (¾″-wide) pre-gathered white
    eyelet trim
1⅓ yards (1″-wide) red grosgrain ribbon
tracing paper
⅓ yard (1″-wide) green satin ribbon
8″ x 12″ piece of gray fabric
5″ x 7″ piece of black fabric
scrap of red fabric
water-soluble marking pen
⅓ yard (1″-wide) pre-gathered white
    eyelet trim
2 (¼″-wide) black shank buttons
black perle cotton
polyester stuffing
¾″ jingle bell

Making the Apron

Note: Use ½″ seam allowance throughout unless instructed otherwise.

1. Fold the polka-dot fabric in half with selvages together and cut 15″ x 24″ piece as shown. (Figure A.) Open out cut piece and cut along the fold for apron front and back. Place front and back pieces together with edges aligned, and fold in half lengthwise; cut as shown. (Figure B.) Cut two 6″ x 8″ pieces for pockets from remaining polka-dot fabric. For lining, cut the striped fabric in the same manner.

2. Pin lining to the apron front (either apron piece), right sides together. Sew sides, shoulder straps, and neck, leaving tops of shoulder straps and bottom of apron open. Repeat for apron back.

3. Turn front and back of apron right side out. Tuck seam allowances inside shoulder straps and press the edges. Butt ends of the shoulder straps (fronts to backs) and slipstitch, first on polka-dot side, then on striped side. Press straps.

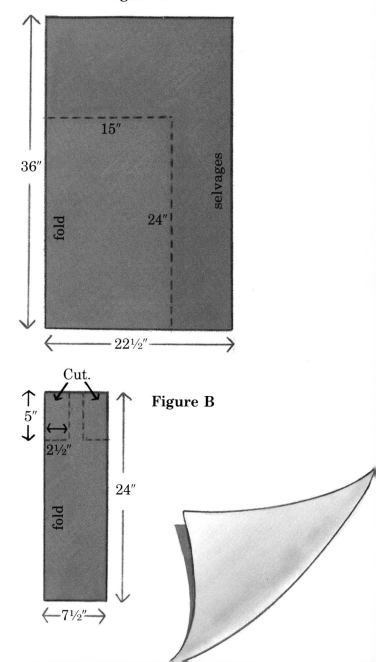

Figure A

Figure B

4. Cut the ¾″-wide eyelet in half. Turn up ends of each eyelet piece ¼″, then ¼″ again, and stitch. On lining side of one shoulder strap, pin straight edge of one eyelet piece to outer edge of strap, pinning the eyelet so that straight edge does not show from the apron front. Machine-stitch eyelet to strap, sewing ⅛″ from the edge. Sew remaining eyelet piece to remaining shoulder strap in same way.

5. With right sides together, pin lining to the pockets and sew, leaving one 6″ edge open. Trim seams; turn and press pockets. Turn raw edges of each pocket to the inside ½″ and press.

6. Turn raw edges of apron bottom (front and back) to the inside and press. With right sides up, pin pockets to bottom corners of the apron front, placing open edges of pockets along bottom edge of apron. Machine-stitch sides and bottom of each pocket, sewing ¼″ from the edges. Slipstitch bottom edges of apron closed.

7. Cut red ribbon into four 12″ lengths. On polka-dot side of apron front, pin one ribbon end to each side edge, 11″ from apron bottom; sew ribbon ends to apron, using zigzag stitch. Sew two remaining ribbons to apron back in same way. Cut free ends of ribbon at an angle.

Making the Appliqué

1. Trace and cut out the patterns. Transfer patterns to fabrics and cut as marked. Using the water-soluble pen, mark placement of ears, antlers, eyes, and nose on the face.

2. With right sides together, pin two ears and sew, leaving opening as marked. Clip the curves; turn the ear and press. Repeat to make second ear.

3. Pin the noses with right sides together and sew, leaving opening as marked. Clip the curves; turn nose and press. Stuff the nose with polyester stuffing and sew the opening closed.

4. Securely tack the nose to the face. Using black perle cotton, embroider one long straight stitch below the nose. Sew on buttons for eyes.

5. Center the face on the apron front. Fold ears in half lengthwise. Position the ears and antlers under the face as marked and pin.

6. Set sewing machine for appliqué. (Consult your sewing machine handbook for best results.) Using satin stitch and gray thread, appliqué the face, leaving opening at the bottom as marked. Lightly stuff the face with polyester stuffing; satin-stitch the opening closed. Appliqué the antlers, using satin stitch and black thread.

7. Turn under ends of the 1″-wide eyelet ⅛″, then ⅛″ again, and stitch. Hand-sew a long running stitch on the straight edge of the eyelet. Pull threads to gather eyelet to 5″. Adjust gathers evenly and pin eyelet along bottom edge of the face. Tack the eyelet in place.

8. Tie the green ribbon into a bow and tack the bow to the apron below the center of the eyelet. Sew the bell to the apron directly below the bow.

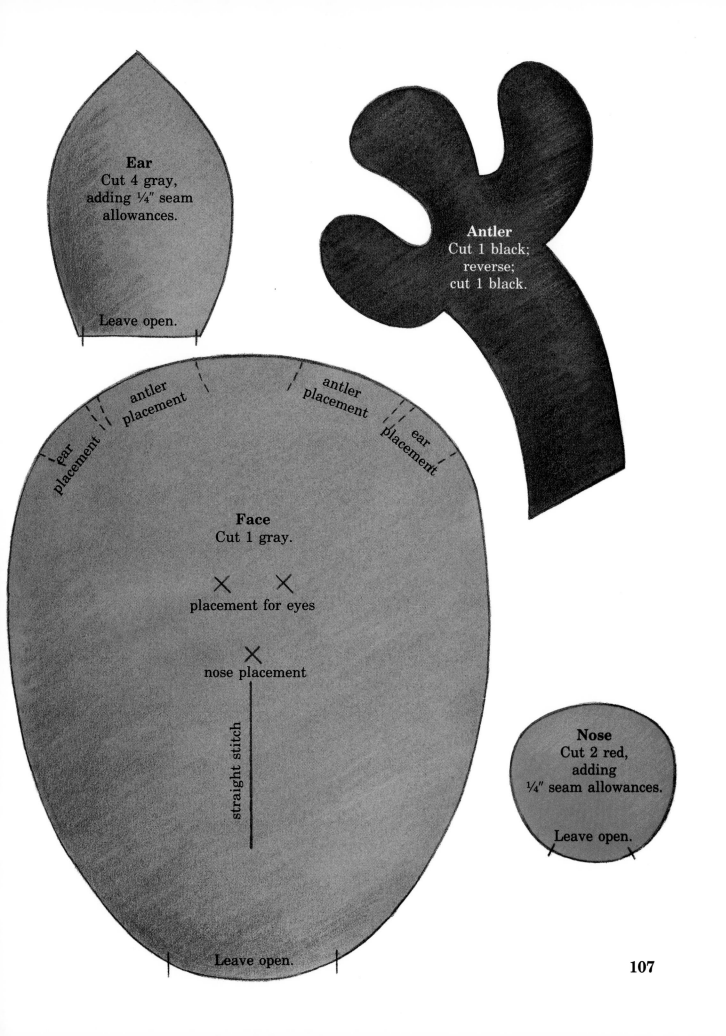

Ear
Cut 4 gray,
adding ¼" seam
allowances.

Leave open.

Antler
Cut 1 black;
reverse;
cut 1 black.

ear
placement

antler
placement

antler
placement

ear
placement

Face
Cut 1 gray.

✕ ✕
placement for eyes

✕
nose placement

straight stitch

Nose
Cut 2 red,
adding
¼" seam allowances.

Leave open.

Leave open.

Jack-in-the-Box Lamp

A little lamplight helps a lot when a tot is at work on a coloring book. Just one piece, the jack and his box are cut from wood and then brought to life with acrylic paint.

You will need:

tracing paper
1 (2-foot) 1 x 6
ruler
electric saber saw
sandpaper
clear acrylic spray enamel
paintbrushes
acrylic paint
carbon paper
4 small apothecary knobs
$\frac{1}{4}''$ electric drill
$\frac{13}{16}''$ paddle drill bit
$\frac{3}{8}''$ and $\frac{1}{8}''$ drill bits
1 ($\frac{3}{8}''$-diameter and 12''-long) figurine pipe
1 ($\frac{1}{8}''$-diameter) I.P. lamp lock nut
2 ($\frac{1}{8}''$-diameter) I.P. knurled nuts
2 ($\frac{3}{8}''$-diameter) washers
5' to 6' electric cord
light socket
2 ($1\frac{1}{2}''$) #8 flat-head wood screws
white glue
grosgrain ribbon (23'' for base plus extra
   for lampshade, if desired)
clip-on lamp shade
light bulb

Note: If you do not have experience in wiring, consult your local lamp and lighting store before attempting to wire the electric cord to the light socket.

1. Trace and cut out the pattern for the jack-in-the-box.

2. On the back (rough side) of the 1 x 6, draw a $5\frac{1}{2}''$ square for the lamp base; draw around the jack-in-the-box. Cut out the wood pieces, using the saber saw. Sand the pieces smooth.

3. On the bottom of the lamp base, mark the center of one edge; measure and mark $1\frac{3}{8}''$ in from center mark. Using the electric drill and $\frac{13}{16}''$ paddle drill bit, drill a hole for the figurine pipe halfway through the base at the $1\frac{3}{8}''$ mark. (This hole will allow you to tighten the lock nut on the pipe.) Using the $\frac{3}{8}''$ drill bit, finish drilling the hole completely through the base. (This hole will provide a tight fit for the pipe.)

4. Apply clear acrylic enamel to jack-in-the-box and base. Let dry and sand lightly. Paint jack-in-the-box and base white. Allow to dry. Using carbon paper and pencil, lightly transfer features to front of the jack-in-the-box. Paint the features and let dry.

5. On bottom of the lamp base, attach an apothecary knob at each corner, $\frac{1}{2}''$ in from the sides.

6. Install the figurine pipe, using a washer and I.P. lock nut on bottom and a washer and I.P. knurled nut on top of the wood base. Tighten the nuts.

7. Thread the electric cord through the pipe and wire the cord to the light socket. Attach the light socket to the top of the pipe with an I.P. knurled nut.

8. On top of base, center the jack-in-the-box between the pipe and the front edge; glue in place and let dry. On bottom of base directly below jack-in-the-box, measure and mark $1\frac{3}{4}''$ from either side of base. At each mark, drill a $\frac{1}{8}''$ hole through the base and the bottom of the jack-in-the-box. Secure the jack-in-the-box to the base with the wood screws.

9. Glue ribbon around the base and shade. Allow glue to dry. Insert bulb and attach shade.

Fishbowl Puzzle

Puzzled over what to give the small fry who live next door? If they're between the ages of three and six, here's one gift they'll all enjoy.

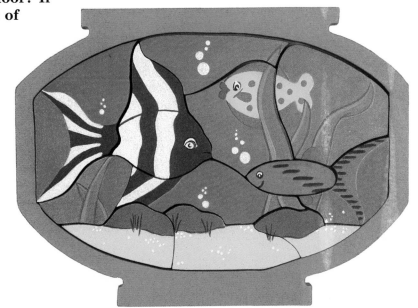

You will need:
tracing paper
1 (16″-long) 1 x 12
carbon paper
ruler
band saw (or jigsaw)
wood glue
12″ x 16″ (¼″) plywood
sandpaper
wood filler
clear acrylic spray enamel
paintbrushes
acrylic paint

1. Trace complete pattern for the puzzle. Cut out the pattern, cutting along the outer outline.

2. On the 1 x 12, draw around the pattern. Using carbon paper and pencil, transfer cutting lines (black lines) for the puzzle pieces. For the puzzle frame (pink fishbowl), draw a ¾″ border around the puzzle; add top and bottom of fishbowl, referring to photograph for shape.

3. Using the band saw, cut along the outline of the frame. Decide the route you will follow to cut the puzzle pieces. Make a cut into the frame and cut out the 12 pieces. When cutting is complete, glue the edges of the frame back together and let dry. Gently sand the edges of the frame and puzzle pieces.

4. For puzzle backing, transfer outline of the frame to the plywood. Using the band saw, cut out the backing. With edges aligned, glue the backing to the frame and let dry; sand the edges. Apply wood filler if needed and sand again.

5. Spray the puzzle frame, pieces, and backing with clear acrylic enamel. Let dry and sand lightly.

6. Assemble the puzzle pieces inside the frame. Using carbon paper and pencil, transfer details for painting. Remove the pieces and paint, applying several coats and letting the paint dry between coats. Paint the frame and backing. Let dry.

7. Assemble the puzzle.

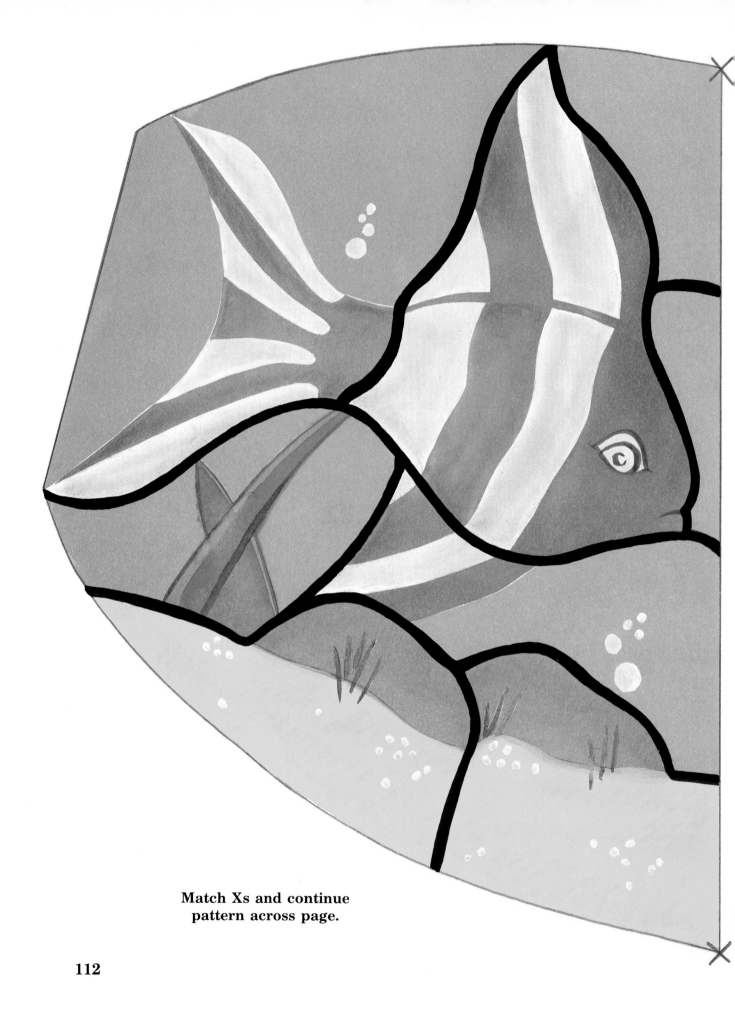

**Match Xs and continue
pattern across page.**

112

**Match Xs and continue
pattern across page.**

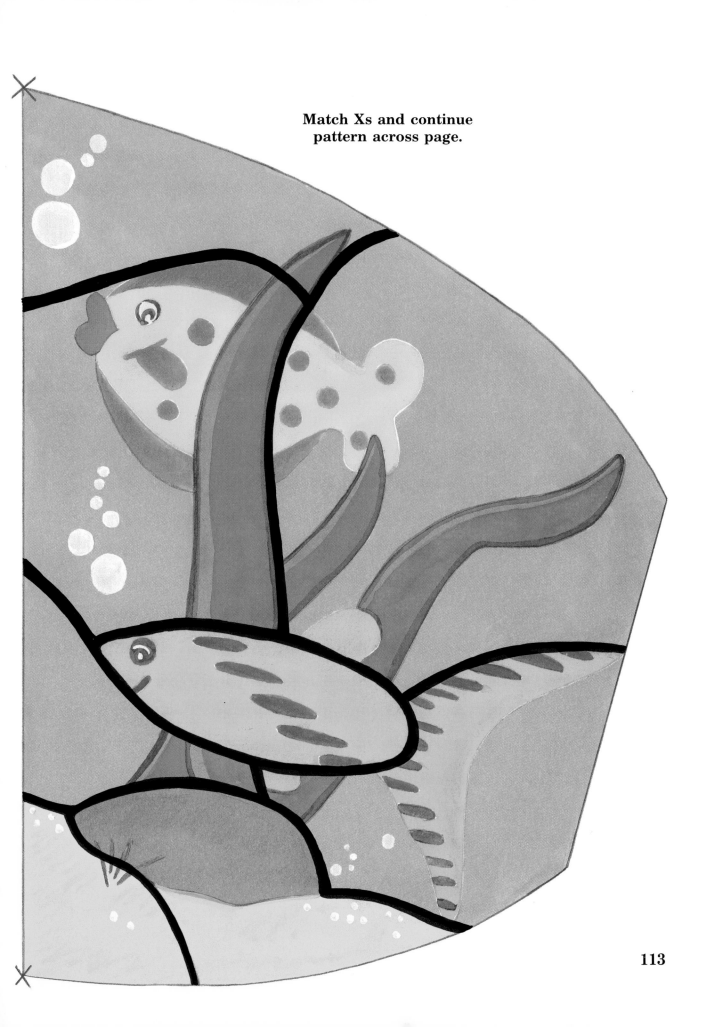

113

Kittens and Mittens

Stitch and stuff one or all of these sock doll kitties. Soft and cuddly, they're "purr-fect" playmates and bedtime buddies.

You will need:
1 (size 10-13) men's dark gray crew sock
1 pair (size 7-8½) boys' white crew socks
l (size 7-8½) boys' black crew sock
polyester stuffing
darning needle (3″ to 4″ long)
heavy-duty thread (gray, white, and
    black)
pale blue and peach yarn
black and pink embroidery floss
stiff quilting thread (for whiskers)
¼ yard each of three different red print
    fabrics
¼ yard white fabric

¼ yard solid red fabric
1 yard (1″-wide) eyelet trim
2½ yards white single-fold bias tape
¾ yard narrow red rickrack (for aprons)
scrap of green felt (for mittens)
¾ yard narrow trim (for mittens)
1½ yards red crochet thread (for mittens)
thread to match fabrics
two (⅜″-wide) red buttons (for overalls)
7 pairs small snaps

Note: Use ¼″ seam allowances throughout the project.

114

Making the Dolls

1. To make the arms, cut socks as follows: for the mama cat, cut 5″ toe section off the gray sock; for the kittens, cut 3″ toe sections off the black and the white socks. Cut each toe section in half along the curve as shown. (Figure A.) Fold each piece in half lengthwise, right sides together, and sew along the curve, leaving straight end open.

Turn arms right side out and stuff firmly. Hand-sew a line of running stitches around each open end, ½″ from the edge. Turn raw edges to the inside and pull thread to close opening; secure the thread.

Figure A

Cut in half along curve.

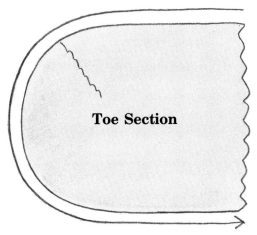

Toe Section

Round off corners.

Figure C

2. To make the ears, cut a 1″ slit along top and bottom folds on the remaining portion of each sock. (Figure B.) Refold the sock to align the 1″ cuts; round off the inside corners by cutting. (Figure C.) Turn the sock wrong side out and stitch raw edge, stretching the sock slightly. Turn the sock right side out and reshape the ears; stitch along bottom of the ears, sewing all the way across the sock, to form top of the head.

3. To make the body, firmly stuff the heel portion (head) and ribbed portion (body). Hand-sew a line of running stitches around the open end of the sock, ½″ from the edge. Turn edges to the inside and pull thread to close opening; secure thread. To form the neck, hand-sew running stitches around the body where the ribbing begins; pull thread gently and wrap around the neck two times. Secure thread and trim ends.

Figure B

←1″→

←1″→

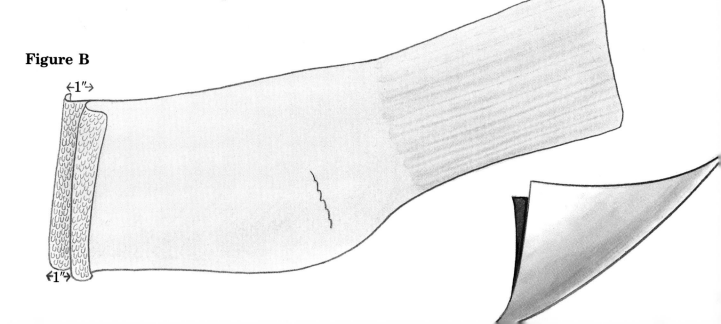

4. Sew the arms to each body approximately 1″ below the neck.

5. To form the face, hold the body with the head at the top and the heel facing you. Thread the darning needle with heavy-duty thread in the same color as the sock. Stitch each face as follows, pulling the stitches snugly to give face a "sculptured" shape:

Secure the thread in the center of the face ½″ below the heel by taking two small backstitches between points A and B. Then push the needle in at A and push out at C. Move across ½″ and push the needle in at D. Push out at B, in at E, and out at F. Move across ½″ and push the needle in at G. Push out at A, in at H, and out at I. Push the needle in midway between points A and B and push out at J. Push in at K and out between A and B. Secure the thread with a small knot; trim the ends. (Figure D.)

6. Using the blue yarn, work either horizontal or vertical satin stitches for the eyes; work three or four vertical stitches with black floss for the pupils. Using peach yarn for the mama cat and pink floss for the kittens, work satin stitches in a V shape for the noses. Work horizontal satin stitches with pink floss for mouths on the kittens.

7. For the whiskers, thread a needle with the quilting thread. Take a small stitch in the cheek area and pull, leaving a 2″ to 2½″ tail of thread; secure the thread and trim 2″ to 2½″ from the knot. Repeat this procedure to make three pairs of whiskers on each cheek of the mama cat and two pairs of whiskers on each cheek of the kittens.

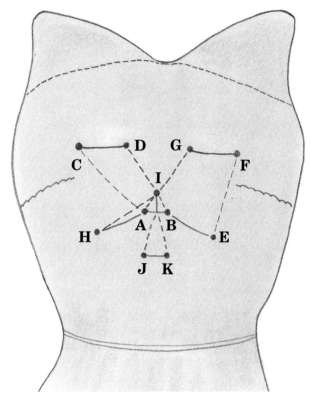

Figure D

Making the Clothes

Trace and cut out the patterns for the clothes; transfer all pattern markings.

Dresses and Shirt

1. From one red print fabric, cut two sleeves, one dress front, and one dress back for the mama cat. From the second red print fabric, cut four sleeves, two dress fronts, and two dress backs for the girl kittens. From the third red print fabric, cut two sleeves, one shirt front, one shirt back, and four collar pieces for the boy kitten. Cut the three dress backs and the shirt front in half along the center fold. With right sides together, pin shoulder seams and sew.

2. Make gathering stitches along the curved edges of the sleeves as marked on the patterns. Pin sleeves to armholes with right sides together and with center marks on sleeves aligned with the shoulder seams. Adjust gathering stitches to fit; sew. Turn right side out. Turn under raw edges of sleeves ¼″ and press; turn under again ½″ and slipstitch. Pin eyelet trim to bottom edge of the mama cat's sleeves, aligning straight edge of eyelet with edges of sleeves; sew.

3. Pin front and back pieces with right sides together. Sew side and underarm seams. To finish back edges, turn edges under ¼″ and press; turn edges under ¾″ and press. Sew.

4. Make gathering stitches along the neck edges as marked on the patterns. Adjust gathering stitches to fit. (A small tuck may be needed to fit dresses around the girl kittens' necks.) On each dress, pin bias tape to the neck edge, right sides together. Sew; press tape to the inside. On the mama cat's dress, slipstitch tape to wrong side of dress neck; pin eyelet to edge of neck, aligning straight edge of eyelet with edges of neck. Sew.

5. For the boy kitten's shirt, pin two collar pieces, right sides together. Sew along the curved edges. Trim seams; clip curves. Turn collar right side out and press. Repeat for second collar.

With raw edges aligned, pin collars to the right side of the neck edge. (The collars should meet in the back over the gathering.) Pin bias tape to remaining neck edge of the collar, right sides together, and sew. Clip curves and press tape to the inside; slipstitch tape to wrong side of shirt.

6. Hem dresses and shirt. Sew two snaps to back of mama cat's dress; sew one snap each at neck of the kittens' dresses and shirt.

Aprons

1. From white fabric, cut one mama cat apron and two girl kitten aprons; cut one 2″ x 20″ strip for mama cat's sash.

2. Pin eyelet trim to the right side of the curved edges of each apron; baste in place. Pin rickrack along straight edge of the eyelet and baste in place. Using red thread, machine-zigzag through all three thicknesses.

3. Sew a gathering stitch along the top of the mama cat's apron. Adjust stitches so that the top of the apron measures 4½″ across.

4. For the girl kittens' aprons, fold each apron to make tucks as marked on pattern. Press tucks away from apron center and topstitch.

5. Finish the long edges of mama cat's sash by pressing edges under ¼″, wrong sides together. Turn edges under ¼″ again; press and stitch. Finish ends of the sash same as above. For each girl kitten's sash, cut one 23″-long piece of white bias tape. Mark the centers of all three sashes.

6. With right sides together and center marks aligned, pin one side of the sash to the mama cat's apron; sew. Fold sash in half lengthwise over the raw edge of the apron. Press sash and slipstitch to the wrong side of the apron.

For the girl kittens' aprons, press each piece of bias tape in half lengthwise. Fold tape over the top of each apron; pin and baste in place, making tiny corners at the top of each tuck. Sew tape to the top edges of the apron, stitching along entire length of the bias tape sashes.

Overalls

1. From the solid red fabric, cut one overall piece, one facing piece, and one 2″ x 14″ strip for the straps.

2. Pin the facing to the overalls, right sides together, and sew. Clip the curves; turn and press.

3. Hem overalls so that 1½″ to 2″ of the boy kitten's "feet" will be below the overalls. With right sides together, pin back seam of the overalls and sew.

4. Fold the 2″ x 14″ strip in half lengthwise, right sides together. Pin and sew, leaving the ends open. Turn the strip right side out and press. Cut strip in half. Pin one end of each strip to the back of the overalls; hand-sew in place. Sew snaps to free ends of straps and to wrong side of the front of the overalls. Sew buttons to right side of front of overalls as marked.

5. Dress boy kitten in shirt and overalls, making sure back seam of overalls is centered on the body. To form legs, thread the darning needle with a double strand of red thread. Starting at the bottom edge of seam on back of the overalls, push the needle straight through to center front. Reinsert needle about ¼″ up and push straight through to the back seam, pulling the thread snugly. Continue stitching in same manner for about 1½″. Secure thread and trim ends.

Mittens

1. From the scrap of green felt, cut six mittens as marked. To make each mitten, sew the curved edges together, leaving the straight edge open.

2. Hand-sew the narrow trim around the open end of each mitten, making a small loop at the seam.

3. Cut the red crochet thread into three 20″ lengths. Thread each length through the loops of one pair of mittens and knot the ends. Hang the mittens around the kittens' necks.

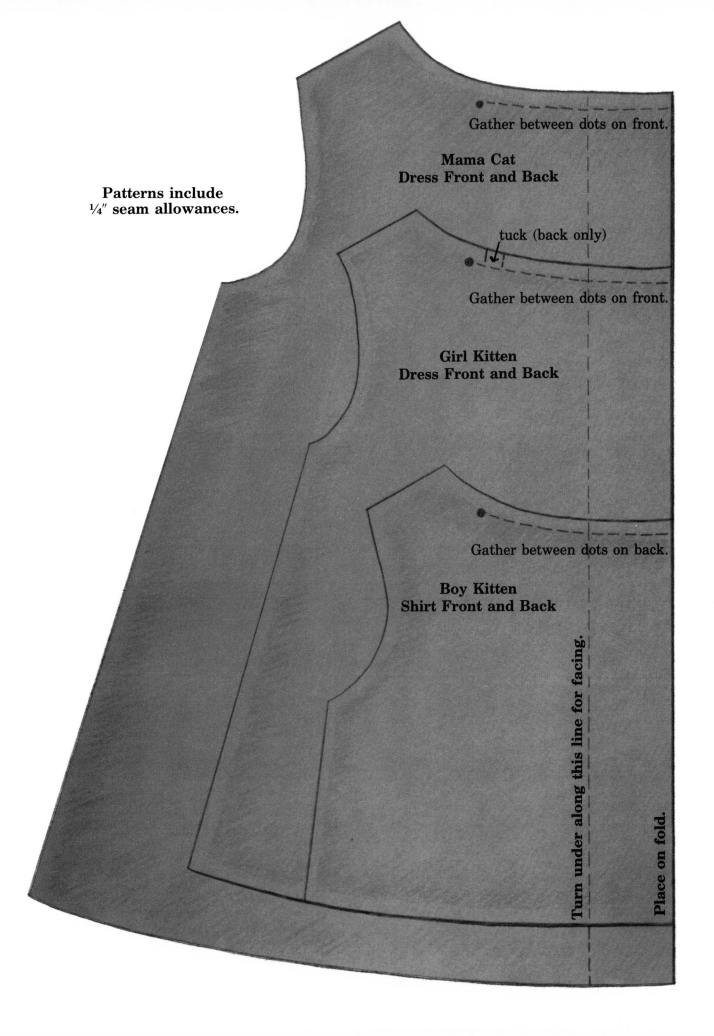

Patterns include ¼″ seam allowances.

Gather between dots on front.

**Mama Cat
Dress Front and Back**

tuck (back only)

Gather between dots on front.

**Girl Kitten
Dress Front and Back**

Gather between dots on back.

**Boy Kitten
Shirt Front and Back**

Turn under along this line for facing.

Place on fold.

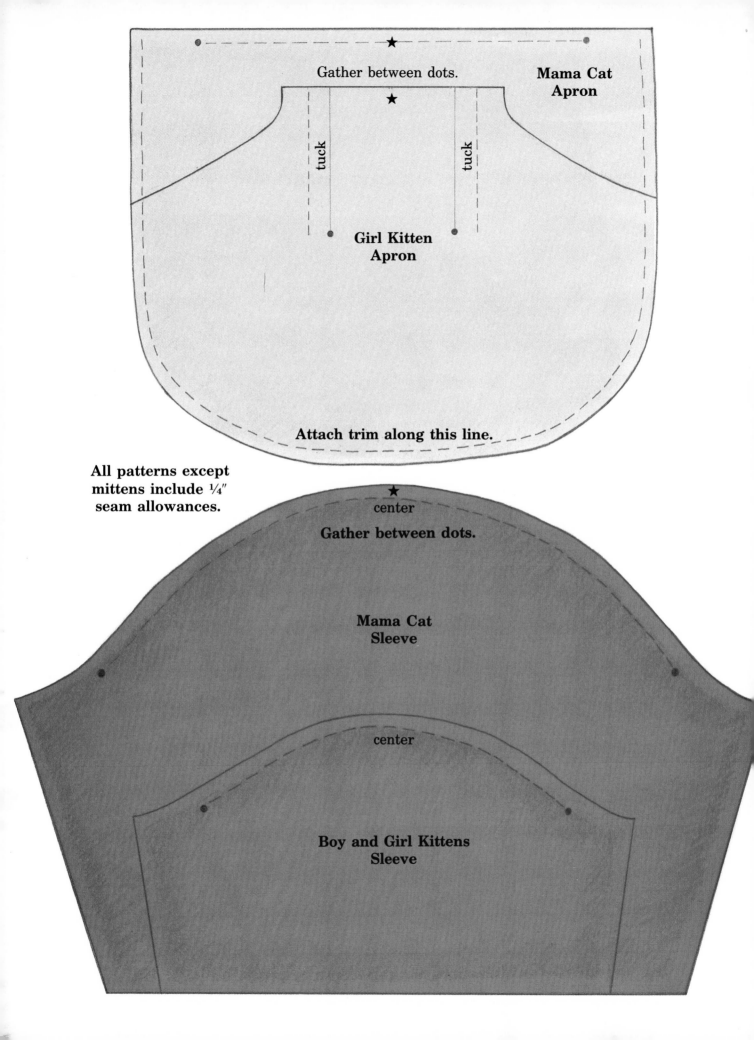

Gather between dots.

**Mama Cat
Apron**

tuck   tuck

**Girl Kitten
Apron**

Attach trim along this line.

**All patterns except
mittens include ¼″
seam allowances.**

center

Gather between dots.

**Mama Cat
Sleeve**

center

**Boy and Girl Kittens
Sleeve**

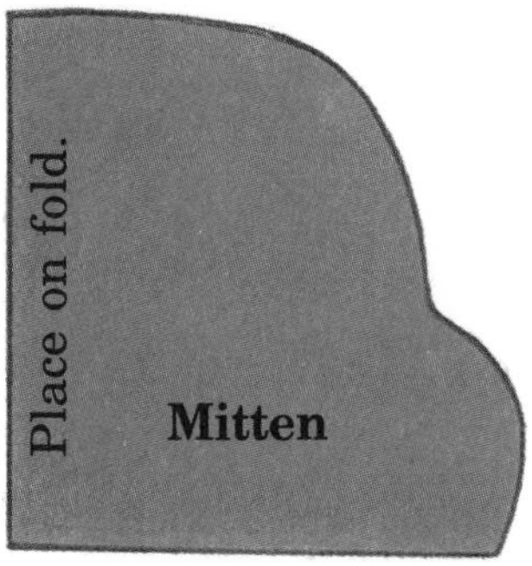

Place on fold.

Mitten

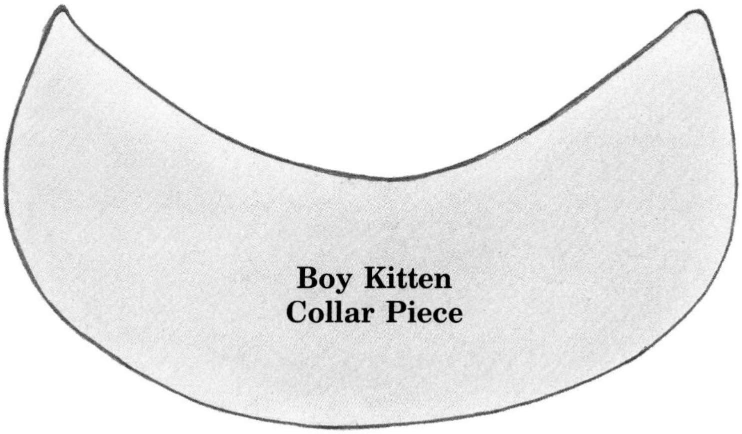

**Boy Kitten
Collar Piece**

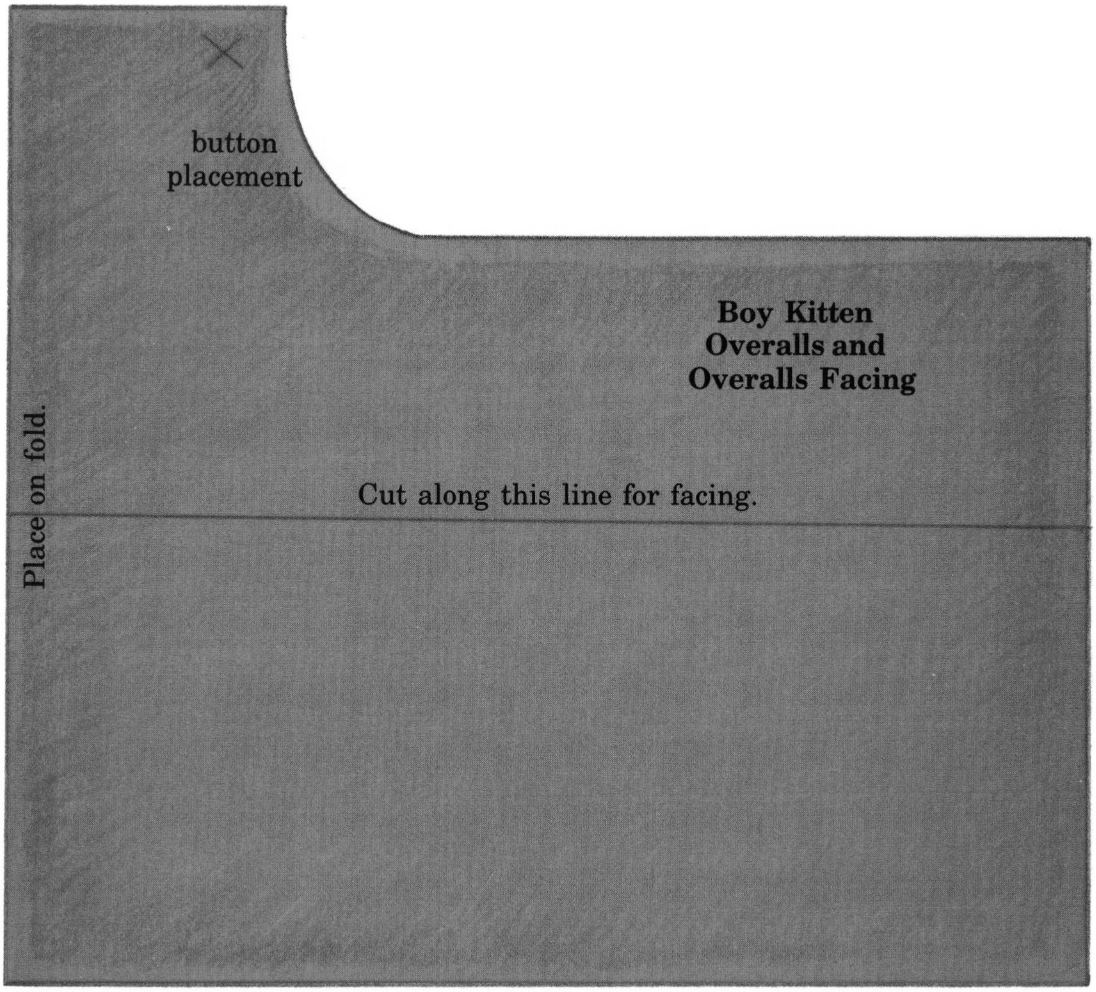

×

button
placement

**Boy Kitten
Overalls and
Overalls Facing**

Place on fold.

Cut along this line for facing.

Pull-Along Pal

There's nothing like having a
friend, who follows wherever you go!

You will need:

tracing paper
ruler
1 (3-foot) 1 x 9
electric saber saw
hole saw (for electric drill)
¼″ electric drill
sandpaper
paintbrushes
clear acrylic spray enamel
acrylic paint (gray, black, white, and
    yellow ochre)
⅛″ and ³⁄₁₆″ drill bits
4 (1″) #10 flat-head wood screws
countersink bit
wood filler
4 (1½″) #10 flat-head wood screws
4 (1¾″) #14 round-head wood screws with
    ¼″ threadless shaft
4 flat washers with ¼″ hole in center
scrap of gold felt for ears
white glue
1 (¾″-wide and 6″-long) piece of black
    "fur"
9 (10″-long) strands of black embroidery
    floss
screw eye
30″ thick white cording
large bead

1. Trace and cut out the patterns for the giraffe. Set the pattern for the ear aside.

2. On the 1 x 9, draw a 6¾″ x 8½″ rectangle for the base; draw around the pattern for the giraffe's body, placing the pattern so that the giraffe's neck runs parallel with the grain of the wood. Position the leg patterns on the 1 x 9, placing bottom of feet along the factory edge. Draw around the legs; reverse the patterns and draw around the legs again.

3. Using the saber saw, cut out the base and pieces for the giraffe. Using the electric drill and hole saw, cut four 2″ wheels,

making a ¼″ hole in center of each. Sand the pieces.

4. Apply enamel to all wood pieces; let dry and sand lightly. Paint the platform gray, the wheels black, and the giraffe pieces white, applying several coats of paint and letting the pieces dry between coats and after the final coat.

5. Place one front leg on top of the other and align the edges; drill a ⅛″ hole through both, as marked on pattern. Repeat for back legs. Drill ⅛″ holes through the body as marked on pattern. Attach the legs to the body with the (1″) #10 wood screws, countersinking the screw heads. Fill holes with wood filler; let dry and sand smooth.

6. Center the giraffe on the base and trace the outline of each foot. In the center of each outline, drill a ⅛″ hole through the base. Glue the giraffe in place and let dry.

  Turn project over. Passing the drill through each existing hole in base, drill a ⅛″ hole in each foot. Secure legs to base with the (1½″) #10 wood screws.

7. On one 8½″ side edge of the base, center and drill a ⅛″ hole, 1″ from the front end; center and drill a ⅛″ hole, 1″ from the back end. Repeat for remaining 8½″ side edge. To attach wheels, pass a #14 wood screw through wheel and a flat washer, and insert screw in ⅛″ hole.

8. Touch up project with paint as needed and let dry. Draw features on giraffe, referring to patterns for placement. Paint the features and let dry.

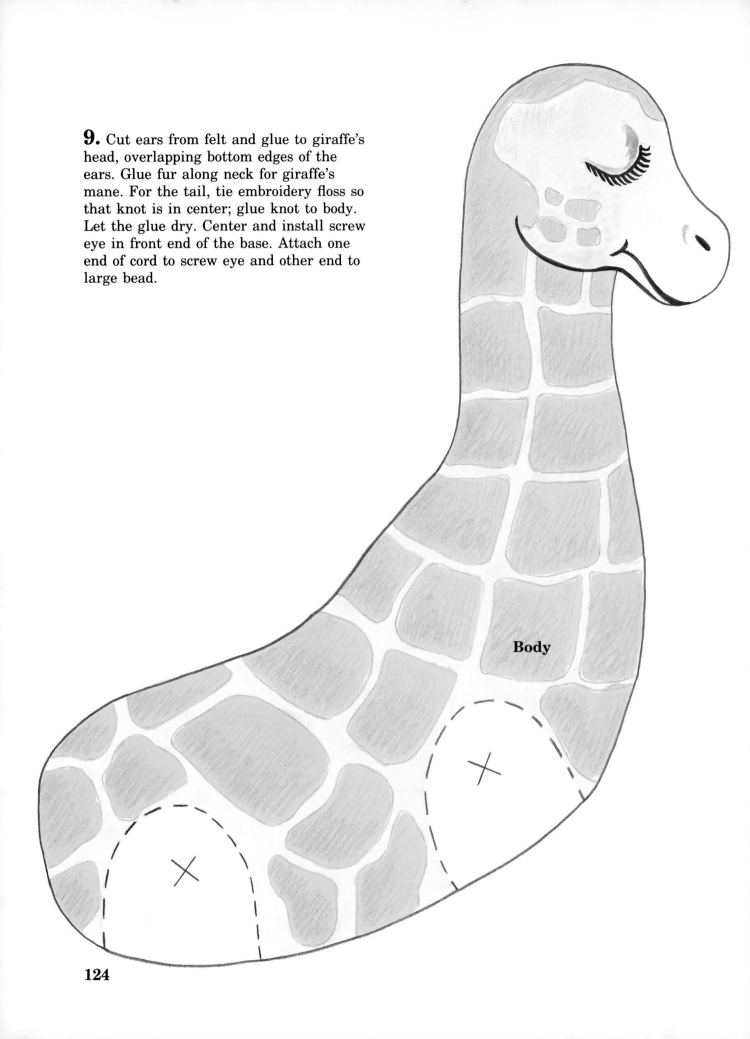

9. Cut ears from felt and glue to giraffe's head, overlapping bottom edges of the ears. Glue fur along neck for giraffe's mane. For the tail, tie embroidery floss so that knot is in center; glue knot to body. Let the glue dry. Center and install screw eye in front end of the base. Attach one end of cord to screw eye and other end to large bead.

Body

124

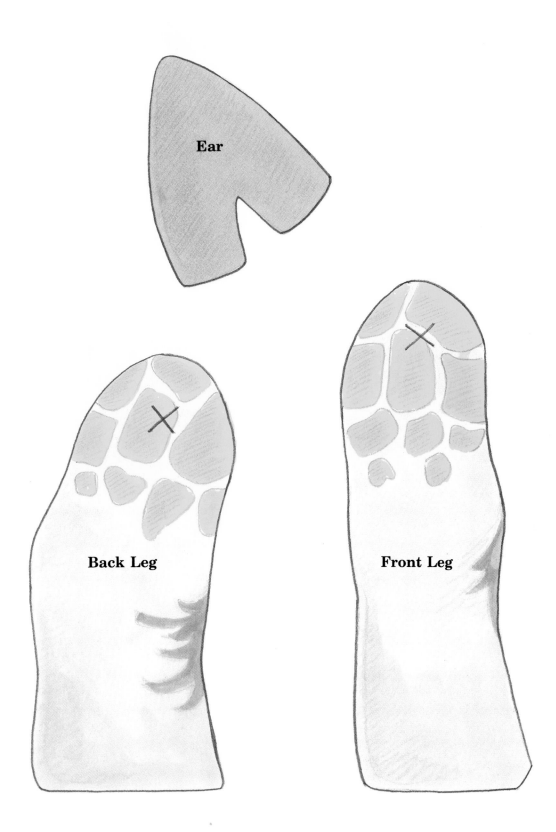

Little Pin Soldiers

Six wooden soldiers standing in a row . . . roll the ball, and down they go! Guaranteed to provide hours of fun, this bowling pin set is quick, inexpensive, and easy to make. (Tape and a steady hand help.)

You will need:
saw
1 (1½″-diameter and 3′-long) wooden dowel
fine sandpaper
clear acrylic spray enamel
masking tape
paintbrushes
acrylic paint (red, blue, yellow, brown, black, and white)

1. Using the saw, cut the dowel into six 6″ lengths. Sand the dowels smooth. Spray with clear acrylic enamel; let dry and sand lightly.

2. On each dowel, mask below the hat line and above the pants line as marked on pattern. Paint unmasked portion of hat red and let dry. Turn dowel upside down and paint pants red. Let dry and remove tape.

3. Mask dowel above neckline and below pants line. Paint shirt blue. Allow to dry and remove tape.

4. Using a pencil, lightly draw all the details. (Pattern is given for glove.) Paint the details, referring to pattern for colors. Allow to dry.

5. Spray the soldiers with clear acrylic enamel. Let dry and spray bottoms.

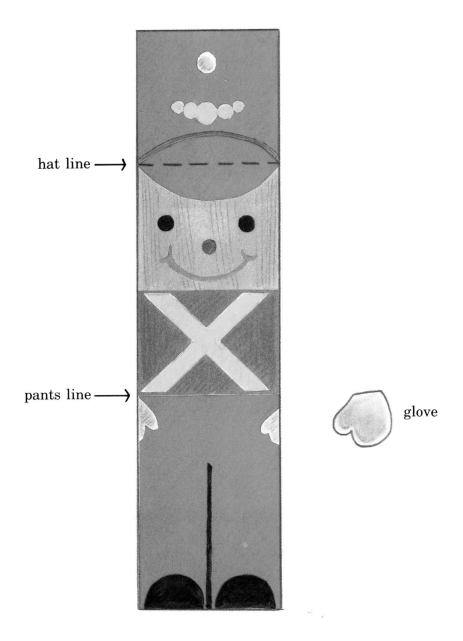

hat line ⟶

pants line ⟶

glove

Sleepytown Clown

This colorfully clad clown will keep kids cozy while they nap, read, or watch TV. Perfect company (nice and quiet), he's a delightful bozo to have around.

You will need:
½ yard (45″-wide) royal blue fabric
1 yard (45″-wide) yellow print fabric
1¼ yards (45″-wide) blue polka-dot fabric
3 yards (45″-wide) quilt batting
1 yard (45″-wide) red fabric
½ yard (45″-wide) green fabric
½ yard (45″-wide) peach fabric
¼ yard red mini-dot fabric
white, black, and red fabric scraps
thread to match

⅔ yard (2″-wide) white eyelet trim
⅔ yard (¾″-wide) red grosgrain ribbon
43″ (1″-wide) Velcro
2 (1″-wide) black buttons
1 pair (½″-wide and 40″ to 45″-long) blue shoelaces
polyester stuffing
3″ x 4″ piece of cardboard
1 skein very heavy brown yarn

Note: Finished size of the bag, excluding hands and feet, is approximately 21″ x 40″. Use ½″ seam allowances throughout project unless instructed otherwise.

Making the Bag

1. From the yellow print fabric, cut two 22″ x 31″ pieces. From the royal blue fabric, cut two 13″ x 22″ pieces. Cut two 22″ x 43″ pieces from the blue polka-dot fabric and three 22″ x 43″ pieces from the quilt batting. Save remaining quilt batting for clown hands.

2. To make the top of the sleeping bag, sew one yellow print piece to one royal blue piece, right sides together, to form a section 22″ x 43″. Press seam open. Repeat for remaining yellow print and royal blue pieces.

   Place yellow print/royal blue pieces with right sides together; place one 22″ x 43″ piece of quilt batting on top. Stitch sides and yellow end, leaving the royal blue end open. Grade seam allowance. Turn right side out; press seams. To form pants legs, lightly mark a 20″ line down the center of the yellow print piece. (Figure A.) Stitch along this line, sewing through all three thicknesses.

3. Enlarge patterns for hands and feet. Cut pieces from fabrics and batting as marked.

4. Place two green hands right sides together. Place one batting hand on top. Stitch around hand, leaving straight edge open. Grade seam allowances; clip curves. Turn hand and press seam. Repeat for second hand.

   Turn raw edges of the royal blue end to the inside ½″ and press. Center the hands along this edge, with seam line on straight edge of hands positioned at seam line between the two royal blue layers; pin. Stitch entire edge.

5. Trim the eyelet to fit across the royal blue end, plus 1″. Turn each end of eyelet under ½″. Pin straight edge of eyelet to royal blue end and stitch.

   Place ribbon over straight edge of eyelet and pin, turning ends of ribbon under 1″. Stitch long edges of the ribbon, sewing both in the same direction.

6. To make the bottom of the sleeping bag, place the two blue polka-dot pieces with right sides together. With edges aligned, place the remaining two 22″ x 43″ pieces of quilt batting on top. Stitch sides and one end, leaving one end open. Grade seam allowances. Turn right side out and press seams.

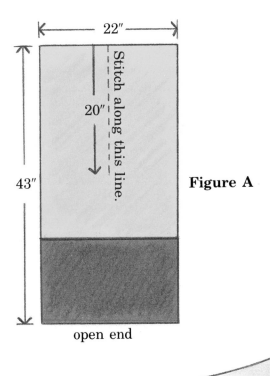

Figure A

open end

7. Sew the two feet pieces, right sides together, leaving the top edge and several inches along the bottom edge open. Clip curves. Turn feet and press seam.

Turn raw edges of polka-dot end to the inside ½″ and press. Center top edge of feet along this edge, with seam line on feet positioned at seam line between the two polka-dot layers; pin. Stitch entire edge.

8. To attach the top and bottom layers of the sleeping bag, pin one piece of the Velcro strip to the underside of the top layer (yellow print/royal blue piece), ¼″ from one long edge. Stitch long edges of the Velcro, sewing both edges in the same direction. Pin matching piece of the Velcro strip to the top side of the bottom layer (blue polka-dot piece), ¼″ from the appropriate edge. Stitch edges of Velcro as above.

Place top and bottom of the sleeping bag together with the Velcro strips evenly attached. Stitch along middle of red ribbon, sewing through all thicknesses and across entire end of sleeping bag. Stitch long open edge of sleeping bag, using a large zigzag stitch and changing thread as necessary to match fabrics. (Figure B.)

9. Stuff the feet firmly with polyester stuffing; slipstitch opening closed. Tack shoelaces in place. (Figure C.) Tie shoelaces in a bow.

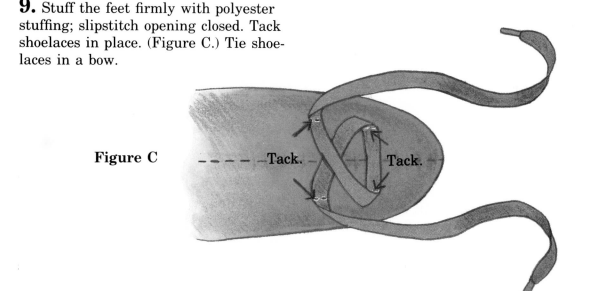

yellow zigzag stitching

blue zigzag stitching

red straight stitching

Figure B

Figure C

Tack.   Tack.

130

Making the Clown Head

1. Trace and cut out patterns for the head, ears, eyes, eyebrows, cheeks, nose, and mouth. Cut pieces from fabrics as marked. From the red mini-dot fabric, cut two 6″ x 13″ rectangles for the bow tie.

2. Pin the clown's features in place on one peach circle (head piece), referring to the photograph for placement. Set sewing machine for appliqué. Using satin stitch and matching thread, machine-appliqué features in place. Sew on buttons to complete the eyes.

3. Place two ear pieces with right sides together; stitch, leaving the inner edge open as marked. Clip curves; turn ear and press seam. Repeat for remaining ear. With raw edges aligned, center the ears on either side of face front; pin.

4. Lay remaining peach circle over the face and ears, with right sides together and ears inside; pin. Stitch, leaving an opening in the chin area for turning. Trim seam; clip curves. Turn head and press. Stuff head firmly with polyester stuffing, maintaining a flat shape. Slip-stitch opening closed.

5. To make tassels for the hair, wrap yarn ten times around the 3″ edges of the cardboard. At one 3″ edge, tightly wrap and tie a piece of thread around the loops; cut loops at opposite edge. Make approximately 19 more tassels in the same manner. Sew the tassels to the seam along top of clown's head, from ear to ear.

6. Center the head on the royal blue section of the sleeping bag top. Tack the back of the head to the sleeping bag in several places.

7. To make the tie, pin the red mini-dot rectangles with right sides together; stitch all sides, leaving opening for turning. Clip corners. Turn tie and press; slip-stitch opening closed. Tightly wrap and tie a piece of thread around the center of the tie. Tack center of tie to back of clown's head and to sleeping bag.

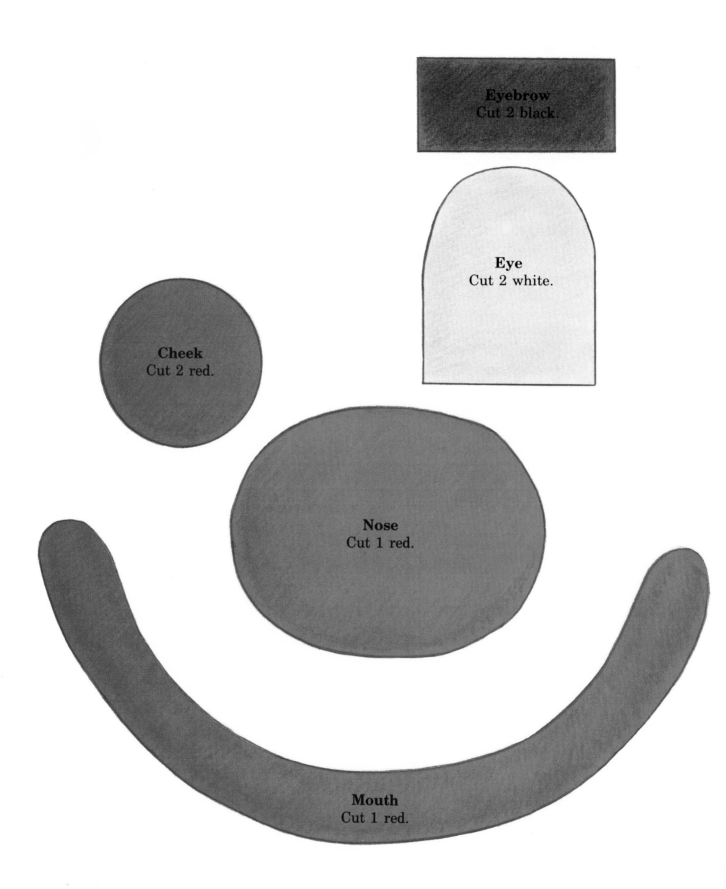

Eyebrow
Cut 2 black.

Eye
Cut 2 white.

Cheek
Cut 2 red.

Nose
Cut 1 red.

Mouth
Cut 1 red.

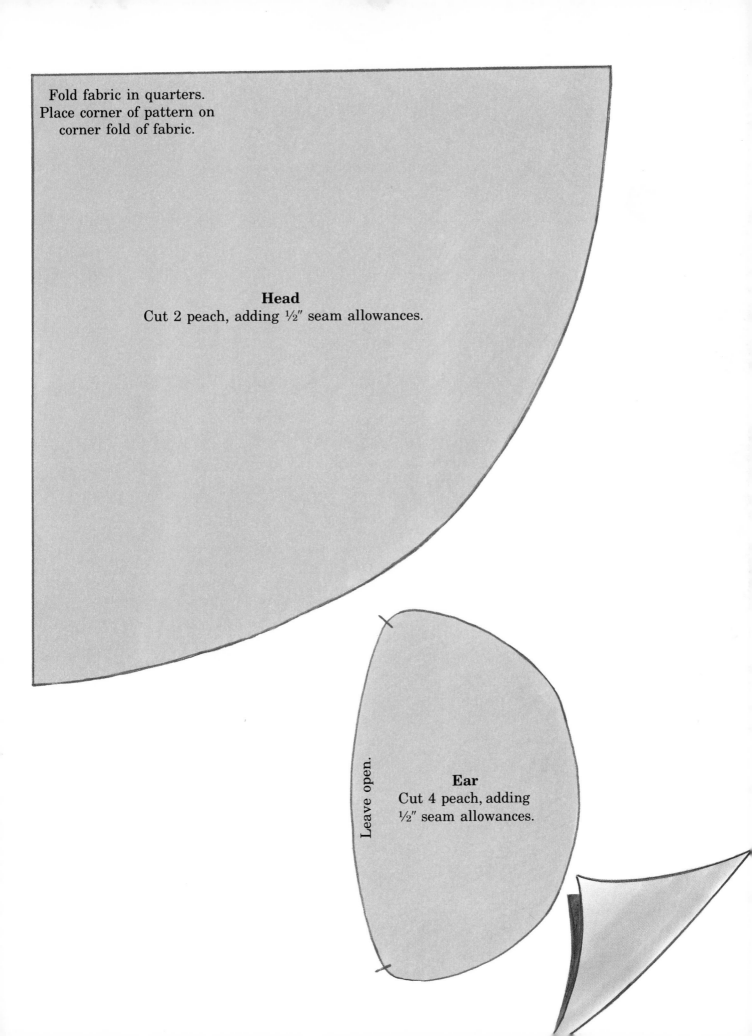

Fold fabric in quarters.
Place corner of pattern on
corner fold of fabric.

Head
Cut 2 peach, adding ½″ seam allowances.

Leave open.

Ear
Cut 4 peach, adding
½″ seam allowances.

Feet
Enlarge, adding ½″ seam allowances.
Cut 2 red.

top edge

Place on fold.

Hand
Enlarge, adding ½″ seam allowances.
Cut 2 from batting and 4 green.

Leave this edge open.

One square = 1″.

Designers & Contributors

Amy Albert Bloom, Little Pin Soldiers, 126.

Peyton Carmichael, patterns for stocking and reindeer cookies, 10; Hobby the Horse, 28; Fancy Frames, 58; Jack-in-the-Box Lamp, 108; Pull-Along Pal, 122.

Sharon A. Christman, Angel Fun, 44; Snow Show, 56.

Karen Clenney, Message Minders, 65.

Hope H. Crawford, Giraffe Overalls, 97.

Florence Dodge, Gingerbread Folks, 22; Frosty Flakes, 26.

Sandy Eichelberger, Snowman Cookies, 13.

Connie Formby, Snappy Wraps, 15-19.

Shirley Foster, Jiffy Gym Bag, 78.

Earl Freedle, pattern for tree cookie, 10.

Miriam C. Gourley, Sew-Easy Bags, 52.

Linda Hendrickson, Pretzel Trees, 16; Holiday Houses, 32; Chummy Bears, 48; Manger Card, 50; Shoe-Choo Train, 84; Noteworthy Suspenders, 100.

Eve London, Candy Canes, 22; Countdown Santa, 36; Paper Candles, 40.

Lee Nix, Book Nook, 82; Ruffled Sweatshirts, 90.

Walter M. Rush, Jr., construction of Jack-in-the-Box Lamp, 108, and Pull-Along Pal, 122.

Kathryn Seifert, Kittens and Mittens, 114.

Kathleen A. Taylor, Satchel Set, 70; Reindeer Apron, 104; Sleepytown Clown, 128.

Carol M. Tipton, Toys Ahoy, 62; Dinosaur Peg Rack, 75; Fishbowl Puzzle, 111.

The Vanessa-Ann Collection, Mary's Little Lamb Collar, 94.

Madeline O'Brien White, Heart Cookies, 12; Lollipop Cookies, 12; Holly Leaf Cookies, 13.

Linda Baltzell Wright, Clay Candlesticks, 66.

Jodie T. Zachow, Holly Leaf Wreath, 43.

Special thanks to the following shops in Birmingham, Alabama, for sharing their resources: **All-Sports Trophy & Plaque Co.; Bair's Ski & Tennis; Benetton/Riverchase Galleria; Blue and White Shops; The Book-Keepers, Inc.; Chocolate Soup, Inc.; Ed's Pet World; Heirloom Shop; The Holly Tree, Inc.; Homewood Sporting Goods; Kiddieland; Lovable Pet Center; New Environs, Inc.; Playfair, Inc.; Ray's Children's Shop.**